Measuring Behavioral Health Outcomes

A Practical Guide

Clinical Child Psychology Library

Series Editors: Michael C. Roberts and Annette M. La Greca

A Continuation Order Plan is available for this series. A continuation order will bring delivery of each new volume immediately upon publication. Volumes are billed only upon actual shipment. For further information please contact the publisher.

Measuring Behavioral Health Outcomes

A Practical Guide

Robert P. Hawkins

West Virginia University
Morgantown, West Virginia

Judith R. Mathews

Munroe – Meyer Institute/University of Nebraska Medical Center
Omaha, Nebraska

and

Laureen Hamdan

West Virginia University
Morgantown, West Virginia

Kluwer Academic / Plenum Publishers
New York, Boston, Dordrecht, London, Moscow

Library of Congress Cataloging-in-Publication Data

Hawkins, Robert P., 1931-
    Measuring behavioral health outcomes : a practical guide / Robert
P. Hawkins, Judith R. Mathews, and Laureen Hamdan.
        p.   cm. -- (Clinical child psychology library)
    Includes bibliographical references and index.
    ISBN 0-306-46080-7 (hardbound). -- ISBN 0-306-46081-5 (pbk.)
    1. Behavioral assessment of children--Handbooks, manuals, etc.
2. Behavioral assessment--Handbooks, manuals, etc. 3. Outcome
assessment (Medical care)--Handbooks, manuals, etc. 4. Child
psychology--Methodology--Handbooks, manuals, etc.   I. Mathews,
Judith R. II. Hamdan, Laureen. III. Title. IV. Series.
RJ503.5.H39 1999
618.92'89'0072--dc21   98-47605
                                                                 CIP

ISBN 0-306-46080-7 (Hardbound)
ISBN 0-306-46081-5 (Paperback)

© 1999 Kluwer Academic / Plenum Publishers, New York
233 Spring Street, New York, N.Y. 10013

10 9 8 7 6 5 4 3 2 1

A C.I.P. record for this book is available from the Library of Congress.

Printed in the United States of America

To our families,
who put up with being neglected
many times during the writing of this manuscript;

and especially to Anthony,
who camped out in his mother's office
on more than one occasion,
waiting patiently for a moment of her attention!

Preface

This book is for behavioral health clinicians who work with children, families, or schools and for those who supervise such work. It teaches how such a clinician can be more accountable to his or her clients, to him or herself, to his or her supervisors, and to managed care agencies who may purchase the clinician's services because of the accountability that his or her data provides. The book comes from our many years of serving clients and teaching others who do.

For years we urged our students and colleagues to regularly collect data on the cases they see. We knew from our own experience that such data, especially when graphed, have several substantial benefits (described in Chapter 1), but we usually had great difficulty getting others to get and use data in clinical practice. Our limited success finally convinced us that we had to accept more responsibility for their frequent failures to get data. We realized that we had not provided sufficient rationale and, especially, sufficient material through which a clinician could learn what to measure, how to measure it, how to graph the data, and how to interpret those graphs. This book is our remedy for that deficit. We hope that it helps clinicians who wish to provide their best service and their supervisors. If for no other reason, clinicians today should measure outcomes in order to be appealing to managed care agencies.

This volume is meant to be a practical manual for use in clinical practice, not a scholarly treatise on scientific method. In order to make the reading smooth, we have limited references and avoided some technical topics that would be relevant if we were discussing data collection for *scientific* purposes (cf. Hartmann, 1982). We have also tried to keep the writing style straightforward and the content simple and practical.

To those who use this book for teaching others or for supervising their clinical work, we should point out that merely reading the manual is insufficient to produce the kind of routine measurement we propose. Instead, we suggest that you also require the learner to practice applying what the book teaches to real cases. This will greatly enhance the learner's fluency at selecting, adapting, and inventing methods for measuring significant behavior. For example, you might require that the learner consider each of his or her cases and select or develop at least two forms—or other methods—for measuring at least two behaviors or environmental events for each case. The forms in the appendix should prove quite helpful. You can almost assure the learner's fluency at doing the measurement if you require the the learner to:

1	justify his or her selection of behaviors to measure;
2	justify the selected method of measurement;
3	describe exactly who is to do what and when in order to get the data, plus what will remind him or her to do it;
4	invent data that might be collected and graph them as he or she would in working with the client;
5	and utilize each of the different kinds of measurement described in the book at least two or three times.

Such training should significantly improve the learner's clinical accountability. In fact, we recommend that you develop your own measurement device, a checklist of the different measurement methods so that you can check off the number of times (and perhaps kinds of cases to which) each learner has applied each method. The list in Table 1 Chapter 3) should help you do this.

We, personally, have found the kind of precise, direct measures described in this book very valuable—far more valuable than tests and other global measures. We hope you do too.

Acknowledgments

We would like to thank all the students and clinicians who have contributed cases and forms to this book. Special thanks goes to John O. Cooper of Ohio State University and Jodi Polaha of Auburn University for reading an early draft and giving us feedback. Thanks also to Vicki Morrison and Diane Ullrich for their help. We would particularly like to thank the many students and clients who posed the problems that led to the solutions described herein.

Contents

Why Get Quantitative Outcome Information on Clients?

This book is for behavioral health clinicians who work with children, adolescents, families, or schools, including clinicians already in practice, graduate and undergraduate students learning to be clinicians, and those who supervise such trainees. For the sake of brevity, reference to "children" in this book will denote any minor from birth through adolescence. The term "clinician," or "therapist," refers to clinical psychologists, school psychologists, social workers, counselors, special educators, psychiatrists, pediatricians, and others whose goal is to help children and their families adjust better; that is, help them come to think, feel, and otherwise behave more adaptively and effectively.

The book is intended to provide practical methods for routinely getting and using quantitative clinical information on outcomes with child, youth, and family cases, although the methods can readily be adapted to adult cases. As will be described later, such information helps in clinical decision making and is often of direct therapeutic value in itself. The information is also very valuable in the supervision of clinicians who are in training or preparing for licensure. Furthermore, as Barlow (1980) predicted, managed care agencies are increasingly requiring evidence of the outcomes achieved by clinicians, and the kinds of clinical information suggested here provide especially credible, precise evidence.

The clinical outcome information described usually involves *direct*, *quantitative* measures of *specific* child behaviors, taken *immediately* when the behavior occurs. These are called "direct observation" data (Cone & Hawkins, 1977) or "direct measures of behavior." Sometimes, however, the information will be measures of events in the child's environment: parent behavior, sibling behavior, teacher behavior, staff behavior, tasks assigned, rewards given, provocations by others, activities offered, and so on.

The outcome information will usually be collected daily or at least once a week, unless such frequent measurement would be irrelevant or infeasible. We will sometimes refer to the information as being "continuous," because it is collected and used as frequently as is relevant and feasible. In sum, then, the clinical outcome information suggested in this book involves direct, continuous measurement of specific behaviors or other events. For the sake of brevity, this book will generally refer to such information as "data," recognizing that the information is not of quite the same quality as that collected in scientific research.

Of course no clinician works without *any* information about the outcomes of his or her efforts. But, generally, clinicians have relied too much on questionable information, such as retrospective reports. Retrospective reports often contain biases and other errors, due to such influences as the client's failure to notice important events when they occurred, forgetting, being unduly influenced by the most recent events, being unduly influenced by one or two salient events, attempting to make things look better or worse than they really are, and trying to please the clinician. In addition, clinicians have often relied on global impressions or subjective judgment. While retrospective reports, global impressions, and subjective judgment all have their values, such information is insufficient in today's world of accountability. The use of such questionable information as evidence of clinical outcome could be compared to a physician's asking a patient to estimate, without instruments, how high his or her blood pressure was five days ago. It is partly due to the excessive use of such questionable information that "The history of psychotherapy is filled with exaggerated claims made by both sincere and insincere individuals regarding the effectiveness, supported by case studies, of their particular form of treatment" (Ogles, Lambert, & Masters, 1996, p. 108). In contrast, the direct, continuous measurement of outcome that we propose here will be far more credible and yield several important benefits.

BENEFITS OF USING DIRECT, CONTINUOUS MEASUREMENT

We can identify three general types of benefits from collecting and using direct, continuous measurement of outcomes: accountability to the child or adolescent, the parents, and oneself; accountability in supervision; and accountability to managed care or other third-party payer. Each will be described.

Accountability to the Child or Adolescent, the Parents, and Oneself

Clinicians are generally quite interested in doing the best job they can reasonably do to help children and their families. This is a main reason for entering clinical professions, and both the client and the clinician will be satisfied when the clinical outcomes obtained from their joint efforts are favorable.

Let us illustrate the "accountability to the child or adolescent, the parents, and oneself" benefit, using a medical example taken from Sperry, Brill, Howard, and Grissom (1996). First, these authors point out that "In the past, outcomes measurement has usually meant measuring a patient's status at the end of treatment and comparing it to his condition when therapy commenced" (p. 22). They then take an example of lung cancer to illustrate how limited such outcome measurement is. Suppose a physician treating lung cancer patients follows a treatment protocol for such cancer and measures how long they live or how much they have improved or declined after six months of treatment. *Eventually* such data can be accumulated and provide a test of the adequacy of that treatment protocol, which will ultimately benefit medical science as a whole and thus future lung cancer patients. However, suppose that someone develops a simple blood test that tells a physician approximately how many cancer cells are present in the patient *today*. This opens up the opportunity of learning how the treatment is affecting *this individual* patient *now*, while he or she is still alive. "Instead of just following protocols, a physician can now monitor a patient daily or weekly to discover whether any cancer cells are present. If the physician is using chemotherapy and the cells are not eliminated, he can immediately switch to another form of treatment (or change the dosage). Care is now more individualized" (Sperry et al., p. 22, parenthetical material added). As Sperry et al. point out, "outcome is feedback. No learning takes place in individuals or in a field without feedback. Further, the rate of learning is often largely controlled by the frequency and utility of the feedback cycle" (Sperry et al., p. 22).

This well expresses our thinking regarding psychological intervention. Continuously collecting and using credible, specific, relevant data on individual clinical cases is essential to a clinician's optimal effectiveness. As Hawkins (1989) points out, such data collection facilitates optimum outcomes in at least six ways:

1 | To get data on specific behaviors, the clinician is forced to specify behavior changes that the child or others in his or her environment need to make. When a clinician and family specify such behavioral objectives, they will focus their behavior-change efforts more precisely. Further, when a parent or child brings in data regularly and the clinician graphs them, as we will recommend later, that helps maintain this focus. A focused, consistent effort will have a much better chance of achieving results than an unfocused, constantly shifting effort.

As any experienced professional can attest, clients can overwhelm a clinician with myriad crises, new problems, and new issues every week, so that the clinical efforts drift vaguely from one objective to another, never achieving any of them. Unfocused efforts not only prevent progress, they often lead to the family's premature termination of treatment, because they do not see convincing evidence of progress. Focused efforts aimed at clearly defined, written objectives make it obvious that the clinician's treatment is truly a teaching–learning process in which there are specific goals to be achieved.

2 | When a clinician defines the necessary behavior changes in writing, it is much clearer to the family what must be achieved in order for things

to improve. This clear specification in itself often produces initial therapeutic gains. Further, designating the child or parent to gather the continuous data keeps that clarity alive.

3 | In the process of gathering and discussing specific data, the clinician usually finds out more about the environment than otherwise. Because the events and conditions in the environment are what produce the child's or adolescent's behavior (along with his or her biological makeup and learning history), knowing the environment is usually crucial to achieving therapeutic outcomes. The clinician will learn the most if he or she observes personally in the child's natural environment, but he or she can learn a great deal even if someone else collects the data and brings them in for graphing and discussion.

4 | The graphed data guide the clinician's behavior. The graph provides visible, durable stimuli that guide the clinician by reinforcing or redirecting his or her therapeutic efforts. The graph is like a report card, except it comes much more frequently and thus is far more helpful. Just as with the earlier example of a physician treating lung cancer, graphed data tell the clinician the "trajectory" of his or her effects, the direction that the outcomes are headed, and their speed of change. Further, graphed data tell how serious the problem currently is.

The graphed data are clear, quantitative, and easy to understand. If the identified problem turns out to be either more or less severe than initially reported—not a rare phenomenon—both the clinician and the family are cued to review just what the problem really is. And if an intervention's results are not satisfactory, the clinician and family are cued to re-evaluate and revise the intervention. The clinician and family, working together, can "tinker" with the intervention over and over, based upon what the data are saying about their success in achieving desired outcomes. The result is a maximizing of favorable outcomes.

Sperry et al. (1996) appropriately refer to this frequent measurement and analysis of the resulting data as "continuous quality improvement, ...the systematic analysis of service quality indicators for the purpose of optimizing service delivery programs and procedures" (Sperry et al., p. 115). This optimization of effectiveness is what the family and clinician both desire.

We should add that when the overall trajectory of results is satisfactory, the clinician and family are encouraged to persist and will not give up easily if there are brief setbacks. Such premature termination of an intervention that actually is working is common (Martin & Pear, 1996, p. 235). So is the opposite error: Clinicians often persist with an ineffective treatment for months or even years. Yet, if they and the family were

5   monitoring graphed data on specific objectives, they would know the treatment is not working and would revise or end it.

5   The processes of deciding what to measure, defining it, and observing or discussing environmental factors encourages analytic thinking and creative problem solving. When an objective is stated that is specific and measurable, it cues the clinician to gather information on possible causes of that specific behavior and to thus perform a *functional analysis*. A functional analysis is a description of the environmental context in which a behavior is functioning, the antecedent and consequent stimuli that may be causing the behavioral excesses, and deficits comprising the adjustment problem (plus some description of relevant learning history). A functional analysis typically leads the clinician rather directly to promising, specific interventions (Hawkins, 1986).

6   A final reason why collecting, graphing, and using data helps make us effective as clinicians is that the graphed data provide tangible reinforcement of our work. The better the outcomes, the more reinforcing the data are. This helps keep everyone enthusiastic and working to achieve better results. In sum, the data are a form of feedback that leads the clinician to maximize his or her effectiveness through repeated cycles: defining specific target behaviors, getting data on those behaviors, graphing the data, evaluating level and trajectory of performance, possibly gathering further information, persisting with or revising intervention, repeating the cycle, and so on.

The more frequent, relevant, credible, and specific the feedback, the more it "teaches" the clinician how well s/he is doing at achieving the objectives of the treatment. It is for this reason that we urge clinicians to obtain continuous—usually daily—data on specific behaviors that are targeted for change during one's assessment and analysis of the case.

Clinicians who neglect to define specific, measurable goals and objectives, design and implement plans to reach those objectives, and then measure progress continuously and graph the data are not providing the best clinical services they can. As a brochure prepared by the Association for Advancement of Behavior Therapy (1991), *What to Expect from Psychotherapy*, states, "... a good therapist will continue to assess a client's problems throughout therapy and change the direction of therapy if needed" (p. 2).

The measurement that we are suggesting has similar rationales to the measurement suggested by Sperry et al. (1996) but differs in two important ways. First, the measurement they recommend is more intermittent, occurring only every few sessions with a client rather than daily or weekly. Second, the data they suggest collecting and graphing come from a *general* index of adjustment, an assessment device that can be applied to a very wide range of clients but is only partially relevant for any one of them. While we consider such a device valuable as part of one's assessment, it is not as sensitive to change as the measurement of specific, individually selected behaviors, which represent the specific objectives set by a clinician for reaching the individual client's clinical goals. Further, a general measure does not have some of the advantages just described, especially the promotion of focused effort. Thus, we urge outcome measurement that is very frequent and specific (cf. Ogles et al., 1996, pp. 108–113), although the intermittent use of more general and inclusive assessments during treatment would certainly provide some additional benefit.

Accountability in Supervision

The second benefit of continuous measurement of specific behaviors accrues from its use during one clinician's supervision of another clinician. During training and subsequent licensure all clinicians are required to be under the supervision of an advanced clinician. If the supervisor relies on the supervisee's impressions regarding a child's progress, the supervisor runs considerable risk of having very inaccurate, vague, and biased information. Further, because families often raise new problems and crises with each visit, the supervisor is likely to have difficulty keeping the supervisee focused enough to reach any specific clinical objectives with the family. For reasons that we have already enumerated, a supervisor would be wise to insist that his or her supervisees write clear goals and the behavioral outcome objectives that will lead to these goals, get continuous data on progress in reaching these objectives, graph these data, and interpret the graphs so as to optimize his or her effectiveness in producing the outcomes selected as important.

Accountability to Managed Care or Other Third-Party Payers

Almost 20 years ago, Barlow (1980) predicted that managed care agencies would increasingly require *evidence* of the outcomes achieved by behavioral health clinicians. Recently, Ogles et al. (1996) reported: "It is becoming more clear everyday (sic) that in the near future health care reform is going to require that outcomes be measured by all health care providers" (p. 112). Similarly, Browning and Browning (1996) state that "... providers will have to demonstrate the efficacy of their interventions in order to remain ... team players with Managed Care" (p. ix).

Ogles et al. (1996)—like most authors on the subject of outcome measurement (e.g., Browning & Browning, 1996; Dornelas, Correll, Lothstein, Wilber, & Goethe, 1996; Edmunds et al., 1997; Johnson & Shaha, 1996; Sperry et al., 1996)—suggest that outcomes be measured through use of some broad-spectrum assessment device. This is probably because such devices are familiar to most clinical psychologists. Ogles and colleagues review several devices that should be valuable for such use. However, applied behavior analysis (see, for example, any issue of the *Journal of Applied Behavior Analysis*) has been developing much more precise and direct measurement methods that yield the six benefits we listed earlier.

We believe that broad-spectrum devices are best used only intermittently, while direct, focused measures are beneficial to use continuously. Managed care agencies should value both kinds of measurement. In fact, we know of one community mental health center in West Virginia where the kind of direct, specific outcome data we recommend are the *only* kind that are routinely collected (on approximately 30% of both child and adult cases), are reported to managed care agencies, and are easily understood and highly satisfactory to those agencies as outcome measures (Michael McDaniel & Michael Mays, personal communication, May 8, 1998). This is consistent with Browning and Browning's (1996) statement that "Case managers want focused symptom reduction" and "...they want results that are measurable within a reasonable number of sessions" (p. 23). Browning and Browning add: "The therapist who knows how to collect outcomes data, and doesn't have to be told to do it but has already undertaken it, will be far ahead of other providers in partnering their work successfully with Managed Care. Providers who routinely do outcomes studies demonstrate their value because they provide concrete data that Managed Care firms can use to justify their existence, hold on to their existing contracts, and win new ones" (p. 146). As Browning and Browning further point out, when Managed Care firms are selecting providers, they will look for persons who can provide credible data that they can use to get and keep contracts.

Unfortunately, like most authors' approach to outcome evaluation, Browning and Browning's approach gives no emphasis on continuous or even frequent measurement, but rather on pre–post-measurement. This benefits the managed care agency and thus helps the clinician obtain contracts with such agencies. Also, as Sperry et al. (1996) point out, it may gradually benefit future clients by improving treatment protocols. It fails to benefit the current client, however, because it lacks the six benefits we listed earlier. For similar reasons it fails to be of significant use in supervision.

QUESTIONS ABOUT DATA COLLECTION AND GRAPHING

Since what we are proposing is quite atypical of what is done in delivering clinical services, there are several questions that need to be addressed at the outset.

Is There No Place for Retrospective Verbal Report?

Of course collecting data on specific behaviors and other events should not replace the use of retrospective recall and subjective impressions. Despite the limitations of such information, it also has advantages. The child and family have usually lived with the problem for a long time and have much historical information that can only be retrieved, however imprecisely, by verbal recall. Also, they are usually the ones who have identified that a problem exists, making it crucial to get their description of the problem, its antecedents, and what makes it a problem.

A second reason to consider using retrospective report is because the clinician's relationship with the child and family will depend in part on how well he or she listens to their account, acknowledges their feelings, and inquires about details. Thus, in most cases, it is essential to take considerable time obtaining the child's and family's reports before attempting to settle on treatment objectives. Further, verbal report can help to identify favorable or unfavorable side effects of treatment, unnoticed problems, and so on.

It should be noted that such retrospective report may differ substantially between the adult and the child. In some cases, this is because of the child's limited cognitive abilities or lack of observational skills, due to a young developmental level. If this is the case, then it is probably wise to have the adult provide most of the information. In other cases, these differences in observations are critical to understanding conflicting perspectives between an adolescent or pre-adolescent child and the parents. In this latter instance, recognizing these differences helps the clinician develop a hypothesis about the presenting problem and sets the stage for collecting quantitative information as a way to help the family gain some objectivity. On occasion, parents' reports also differ. It would then be very important to have both the parents and the child collect quantitative information in order to avoid the perception that the clinician is interested in only one of the perspectives.

Are There Other Kinds of Data I Should Get?

As mentioned earlier, a broad-spectrum measure would be worth using intermittently, or at least pre–post-treatment. Alternatively, Meyer and Janney (1989) point out additional kinds of measures that are not only very easy to get but add substantially to the kind of data we will describe in this book. The measures we will describe are intended to assess the most *direct* effects of one's interventions, which are primary, but any clinician is actually interested in more than these effects. He or she should often be interested in how well the behavior changes generalize to new situations and persons; what positive or negative side effects accrue from the treatment; and how satisfied the child, family members, and others are with the effects. A clinician may also be interested in how the behavior changes affect the child's social relations or how the behavior changes affect where the child is placed to live or for schooling (cf. Fabry, Hawkins, & Luster, 1994).

Meyer and Janney (1989) also point out that a clinician can easily construct simple ways to measure such indirect effects. For example, they illustrate a daily log on which a school teacher can rate what kind of day the child had overall, using a five-point scale, and how well the child did in general. Then the teacher can comment on the day's events and the student's behavior, noting any incidents that seemed important; describe any activities the child especially enjoyed; and describe activities the child did not enjoy. One advantage of such logs is that they are so open-ended that they often provide the clinician with insights not available from an interview or from specific, direct measurements. This might include insights about the family's or teacher's activities, their attitudes, the child's preferences, and such. The disadvantage is that such logs are unlikely to be very sensitive to changes in the behaviors that the clinician and the family have selected to change, so they do not quickly tell how well treatment is succeeding. It is also likely that what will be recorded is highly subject to such factors as the data collector's mood, values, feelings toward the child, and opinions about what should be done for the child. Furthermore, logs can be quite time-consuming and consequently may only be kept sporadically, when there is a problem. Nevertheless, the benefits of such measurement usually outweigh these shortcomings. Although logs will not be described in this book, they can be useful in both planning and evaluating treatment.

A second example of data collection that Meyer and Janney (1989) describe involves inspecting existing records, such as drug dosage records, notes between home and school, or hospital records. A third example is what Meyer and Janney call "incident records," where a teacher, parent, or staff member in a program makes a written record of *any* behaviors that the child shows and that seem especially important (usually problematic). A record is made only if such an "incident" occurs. The person making the record describes not only the significant behavior but also what happened immediately before and after the behavior. This can be very useful, and later we will describe using such recording at the beginning of a clinician's involvement with a case.

Another useful way to collect clinical information is simple but systematic client satisfaction ratings, as suggested by Wolf (1978). According to Edmunds et al. (1997), this is one of the two most frequent measures of a clinician's or agency's performance (the other being ratings by the service provider). The clinician can ask members of the family (and even teachers) to rate their satisfaction with one or more of the following: the goals of the treatment, the specific behaviors targeted for change, the kind of treatment procedures proposed or used, and the results of the treatment. As Hawkins (1991) points out, such measurement can have several benefits: suggesting the need for explaining things further to the family, discovering resources not previously noticed, suggesting promising adjustments in procedures, predicting or detecting undesired effects, assessing the comprehensiveness of the effects obtained, documenting a program's effects on numerous clients in a uniform way, and good public relations. Generally, it is best to get the ratings repeatedly, such as once a month, and it is usually valuable to discuss them with the persons providing the ratings.

By Asking for Data, Are the Clients Then Participating in Research (and Subject to Internal Review Board Approval)?

Quantitative clinical information is not the same as research, in the scientific sense (Hawkins & Hursh, 1992). Instead, it implies that the clinical service has focus, precision, objectivity, and accountability. Most clinicians want a picture of the problem before intervention and asking for baseline data serves this purpose. In fact, the community mental health administrators mentioned earlier routinely get baselines, even if they have to accept the verbal estimates of clients to do so (McDaniel & Mays, personal communication, May 8, 1998). However, unlike scientific research, the primary purpose of quantitative clinical information is to provide good service (and evaluate its efficacy), not to advance science. Nonetheless, the collection of accurate information may in fact turn out to be of such clinical interest that it becomes publishable. Internal Review Board approval is usually sought after the fact to obtain permission to report the results, not to collect the information in the first place.

Why Doesn't Every Clinician Get Data Then?

In spite of the above reasons for collecting data, it is not common practice for a number of reasons (Carter, 1983). The primary reason is probably that data collection is not taught to most human service providers as a routine part of clinical training. Consequently, in training programs, data collection is usually associated with experimental research rather than clinical practice. Because the type of data collected for scientific research are usually not necessary or feasible in a clinical setting, educators may not consider the clinical values of collecting less sophisticated data.

A second probable reason for the rarity of routine data collection in clinical practice is that, in the past, most employers and third-party payers have not required (or reinforced the use of) clinical data collection. However, with the rapid onset of managed care and the move towards brief therapy, those clinicians who can objectively demonstrate change in their clients are at a distinct advantage and may be more likely to be included on provider panels and kept on staff. In addition, with increased accountability, it is not unreasonable to expect that expert witnesses are increasingly likely to be viewed as more credible if they are able to provide clear data to support their testimony.

PURPOSE AND ORGANIZATION OF THIS BOOK

The goal of this book is to provide the clinician with the tools to: (a) measure important target behaviors (and perhaps other events) continuously in most clinical cases; (b) use the resulting data to optimize clinical effectiveness with each child and family; and (c) use the data as part of any presentation of a case—whether to the child or family, in a case conference, to a supervisor, to a colleague, to a managed care agency, or to others. Finally, it is hoped that clinicians using such quantitative clinical information will set a model for other clinicians, convincing them that they, too, should get and use objective, precise data on behaviors and environments in their clinical practice, thereby setting a new standard of accountability and effectiveness.

Although every topic discussed in this book is probably covered to some degree elsewhere (e.g., Alessi, 1988; Barlow, Hayes, & Nelson, 1984), it is the purpose of this book to provide a practical guide for getting and using quantitative information as a part of routine clinical practice. Each chapter presents basic information along with case illustrations. Chapter 9 presents four cases of increasing complexity to illustrate the ongoing and changing process of data collection. While case examples are based on actual cases or compilations of several cases, the data or format may have been adapted to make our points clearly. It is hoped that the reader will attend more to the means of data collection and their implications for treatment than to the specific details of either the data or the intervention method.

The appendix provides the reader with samples of the forms used throughout the text, which may be copied without permission unless otherwise indicated. When appropriate, sources of forms have been acknowledged; however, most forms have been either developed by one of us or handed down from one clinician to another.

Finally, every method, every data collection form, and every graphing procedure presented can be adapted. Each of them was "invented" by one of us or by another professional. The clinician should plan to be assertive and creative—becoming the "inventor" of methods adapted to his or her cases.

Targeting Behaviors to Measure and Change

The first tasks of clinical services are to establish rapport and a therapeutic alliance with the child and family and to find out the general nature of the problem and its severity. Then the clinician and the family need to come to an understanding about how assessment and treatment will proceed, a process that will be especially important if one is to gather data as we are suggesting.

FIRST TASKS OF CLINICAL SERVICES

Establish Rapport and Clarify Expectations

Any good clinician will exert considerable effort in gaining rapport and a therapeutic alliance with the parents and the child at the outset. It is beyond the scope of this book to provide extensive guidance on this topic, but Chapter 6 will discuss it somewhat further and the reader is referred to the many therapy handbooks that address this important topic (e.g., Cormier & Cormier, 1979; DiGiuseppe, Linscott, & Jilton, 1996; Wright & Davis, 1994)

At the same time, the clinician needs to find out what the parents and child expect to happen in therapy. For example, it is common for parents to bring a child to a clinician to be "fixed," much like one takes a car to a repair shop or a sick child to a physician. Many parents expect little involvement, other than providing information. The clinician should work with the parent and child to arrive at an agreement about what their roles will be, how long treatment might last, and what will determine its success or failure.

Another common misconception among parents is that therapy consists of nothing but talking, as they may have seen on TV or read about. While that is true in the treatment of some adult problems and even some adolescent problems, few problems of younger children can be adequately treated that way, and parents need to understand this. One thing that very few parents will expect is for the clinician to ask them to collect data.

Explain the Importance of Collecting Quantitative Information

It is crucial that the clinician and clients come to an understanding about collecting quantitative information if the benefits outlined in Chapter 1 are to be realized. Data are central to determining whether treatment outcomes are being achieved. The following is an example of an explanation given to parents:

> In order to help your child, it is important that we get an accurate picture of the behaviors that you have mentioned, when they occur, and under what circumstances. We may be able to observe some of the behaviors in the clinic—and indeed we may make a special effort to do so—but if we are to realistically detect how effective we're being in treating those behaviors, we must get regular, accurate reports from people who are in the home, school, or neighborhood, where your child actually spends his or her life. The person collecting information for us needs to be part of the child's daily environment and be willing to keep us well informed in as objective a manner as possible. Most of the information will be designed to provide us a daily picture of how well the child is doing. Recording this information daily can be inconvenient and consequently it requires that the recorder be truly invested in the long-term benefits that will hopefully come from therapy.

After giving this explanation, the clinician should ask the parents whether they have such an investment.

Getting Started Collecting Quantitative Information

When the clinician and family seem to have a common expectation regarding assessment and treatment—usually in the first session, but sometimes it takes longer—the clinician should start one or more members of the family collecting data on one or more behaviors and/or environmental events that appear to be relevant to a more complete understanding of the severity, components, and causes of the problem. These initial data will help determine more accurately what needs to be done about the problem and what steps should be given priority (Martin & Pear, 1996), while subsequent data are primarily for evaluating the effects of intervention. It is often a fatal flaw to wait until target behaviors have been selected before collecting data, unlike in experimental research. Collecting data and selecting behavioral objectives should go on concurrently, because the data—along with supplemental information that one discovers while gathering the data—assist in deciding on those objectives.

The ideal way to collect these initial, explorative data is for the clinician to observe in the natural environment for at least two or three sessions—that is where the problem really exists and observation allows the clinician a familiarity with both the behaviors and the environmental context with much greater fidelity and detail than any number of interviews could provide. However, a clinician may not have the luxury of making home or school visits. Furthermore, by necessity, the sample would usually be from only a small fraction of the total situations where the problem exists. Consequently, two other means are usually used to collect the data, and one or both of these should be a standard part of assessment.

The first is systematic observation in the clinic. Many clinicians try to simulate, in the clinic, the situation or situations that they believe may be relevant to understanding the case, doing direct clinical observations themselves in that setting. This is particularly useful if the clinician wishes to manipulate the conditions in order to determine the variables that contribute to the behavior (e.g., analogue situations to determine the functioning of aggression or noncompliance; see Hembree-Kigin & McNeil, 1995; McFall, 1977). However, there are drawbacks to clinic observations. First, it is impossible to simulate the context fully, including stimuli that the parent may not recognize as contributing variables. Second, even if the context can be simulated to some degree, it is not unusual for the child to behave differently simply because the situation is still quite different from the situations in his or her natural environment. Usually, such clinic observations are preceded with assurance to the parents that we recognize the limitations of the setting and do not always see the behaviors they have described.

The second approach to collecting the data is to have someone in the natural environment do it. Not only does this provide more opportunities to collect samples of behavior across settings, time, and people, it also sets the stage for those individuals to begin taking responsibilities for a large role in the treatment.

DETERMINING WHO SHOULD COLLECT QUANTITATIVE INFORMATION

In this book we will refer to the persons who collect information as "data collectors" or "observers," whether they be a parent, a teacher, the child identified as the target by referring persons, a sibling, a schoolmate, the clinician, or someone employed by the clinician. It is important to include all involved individuals, whenever possible, as collectors of at least some of the data, for reasons listed later in this chapter. The persons designated to collect data will be determined by several factors: (a) the setting where the behavior occurs (e.g., the parent at home, the teacher at school); (b) the accessibility to the information (e.g., the parent who is present when the child is getting dressed in the morning or the specific teacher who is doing playground duty when the child tends to be aggressive); (c) the type of information (e.g., only the child can *report* subjective ratings of pain or fear, but the parent can *record* the rating as well as compliance with practice of the exposure step practiced at home); (d) the required awareness of the person being observed (e.g., the parent may be asked to record unobtrusively when a child with selective mutism speaks if it is likely that she will stop speaking when observed; or one parent may be asked to count praise statements in the other parent unobtrusively so that the observed parent does not change his/her behavior due to the knowledge of being observed); and (e) the motivation of the possible data collectors to see changes in the targeted behavior (for instance, a parent may be highly motivated to have a child sleep in his own bed, while the child may not see the importance of changing this and thus may not be a good observer).

In most instances, the relevant adults will be the primary observers, but this is not always the case. All but the youngest children should usually be included in data collection at some level. In this way, the child gets the clear message that this behavior is important and gets immediate feedback. Sometimes children who have a clear idea of the benefits (e.g., rewards) of achieving a goal will prompt the parents and essentially keep the intervention going even on days that are busy for the parents.

Even young children, who may not have the skill or the motivation to do self-recording, can often participate. For instance, if pictograms are used to indicate tasks accomplished (e.g., elements of the morning routine), a child may participate by placing a check mark or sticker in the appropriate square.

Children of school age and older may be directly involved or fully responsible for collecting information, but they should be supervised in doing so. For instance, a 9-year-old might keep a simple graph of soil-free days or a chart of the number of minutes the piano was practiced daily. In these instances, a parent will need to be closely involved to ensure that the data are accurate and to give frequent positive feedback for accomplishments. A pre-adolescent child might be able to record data on a habit (e.g., the number of tics in a 5-minute interval) with parent supervision. (In this example, self-recording might actually be part of the intervention by making the child aware of the habit).

Adolescents can often collect data independently—again, depending on their motivation to make changes. In fact, for some adolescents it is best to have a minimum of parental involvement in order to avoid conflict, which can undermine the treatment. For instance, one adolescent with an anxiety problem was asked to record whether she practiced progressive muscle relaxation each evening and to rate her anxiety before and after her practice. Because of a history of parent–adolescent conflict, the parents were specifically asked not to check on her to see if she was practicing. Although there was no "reliability check," the girl's improved ease in decreasing heart rate in the clinic suggested that she was reporting accurately.

The following guide is suggested to help establish the collection of data as an expected part of assessment and treatment.

GUIDE FOR GETTING CHILDREN AND PARENTS STARTED COLLECTING QUANTITATIVE INFORMATION

Start Right Away

Part of the first session with a family should be used to get one or more members of the family to begin collecting quantitative clinical information. Although there may be only a sketchy idea of the problem during the first session, initiating data collection immediately does at least five things:

1	It helps the clinician to understand the child and family behaviors involved in the problem and how severe they really are, so that appropriate target behaviors and interventions can be selected.
2	It helps the clinician to understand the family's routine, values, and ways of responding to the child, all of which will be very useful in the analyzing the problem and implementing a realistic intervention.
3	It teaches the family, from the beginning, that measurement is part of treatment and that treatment consists largely of getting them to behave differently in their natural environment, not merely of their venting the emotions or gaining "insight."
4	It teaches the parents that the clinician will expect them to carry out "homework" tasks, focus on specific behaviors of their own or their child's, and keep focused during treatment sessions.
5	It may indicate how well the child or parents will keep commitments.

In fact, postponing data collection until the clinician is sure about the target behaviors may implicitly teach the parents that measurement, homework, and focus are not important. As will be discussed later, lack of adherence with this first assignment does not necessarily imply lack of commitment, but it does raise questions about the likelihood of being effective, and it certainly limits the clinician's knowledge of whether he or she is being effective.

The following is a simple explanation that can be used to request initial data collection from a parent. A similar explanation may be used with an older child or adolescent:

Initially, we need to find out more about your child's behavior and the situations in which it usually occurs. This will help us to decide what to work on and how. We know that collecting the clinical information we need can be time-consuming, and so we want you to be sure to tell us if what we are asking is reasonable for you to follow through with consistently and accurately. What we are trying to get is snapshots of the behavior over the next week. Later, we will probably change what information we ask you record; but for now we just need to get a clearer picture of the problem so we can set our goals and objectives and decide how to reach them.

Assuming the relevant family members agree, the clinician and family should then agree on one or more behaviors that seem likely to be important and at least a minimal definition of those behaviors. Then they will need a bit of training in collecting the data, as we will describe later.

Starting with ABC Recording

Sometimes it is best, in this initial assessment phase (as opposed to the "monitoring progress" phase, where the same data are collected each day to evaluate progress, as described by Hawkins [1979]), to have the data collector start with what is called *ABC recording*. This is done when a particular behavior is clearly the problem, yet it is unclear what environmental variables may be influencing that behavior. Because it is for assessing environmental influences, ABC recording involves quite intensive observation, making it too time-consuming if one only wishes to find out such things as how often or how intense the behavior is. ABC recording emphasizes qualitative factors rather than quantitative, in that it helps identify environmental events that influence the behavior. ABC recording is a narrative of the antecedents (the "A" in "ABC") to a particular behavior, the behavior itself (the "B"), and the consequences ("C") that may influence the likelihood of that behavior's recurrence. The observer watches the child for an agreed-upon amount of time and, when the target behavior occurs, records that fact along with what environmental event preceded it and what environmental event followed it.

Figure 1 shows an example of an ABC form, adapted from O'Neill, Horner, Albin, Storey, and Sprague (1990). In this case, the referral problem was projectile vomiting by a 3-year-old child with Down Syndrome, who had a gastric tube for feeding and received continual oxygen through a canula in his nose. The vomiting, which could occur several times in succession, was compromising his nutrition and required immediate clearing of the canula. It was felt that the vomiting was not related to his fragile medical condition or to the timing of his tube feedings. However, given the complexity of this child's condition, the physician was requesting help in determining whether or not the vomiting was a learned behavior. The first step was to ask the parent to make a record of the time and number of vomiting episodes by placing a tally on paper for each episode.

NAME: Earl BEHAVIOR(S): Vomiting + gagging/coughing

INSTRUCTIONS 1. TOP COLUMNS: Fill in specific targeted BEHAVIORS, ANTECEDENTS (e.g., location, activity, persons present, type of instruction) and CONSEQUENCES (e.g., positive rewards/socials, negative consequences such as time-out/reprimand) & COMMENTS (other specifics).
2. EACH TIME THE TARGETED BEHAVIOR OCCURS, write in date & time; check all columns that apply.

Date	Time	BEHAVIOR (Frequency) Vomit	gag/cough 4	ANTECEDENTS (before) Leave house	Enter school	Enter appt.	Eating	Tube Feed	Meals	gag/cough	CONSEQUENCES (after) No school	Late to school	Change clothes	Reprimand	Stay home	Run after T.V.	COMMENTS Cried when saw coat
8/4	8ᵃᵐ	IIII		✓					✓			✓	✓			✓
8/?	8ᵖᵐ						✓	✓	✓			✓				
10?		I									✓					
8/?	8ᵃᵐ	III		✓				✓	✓				✓	✓		✓
2?		II		✓				✓	✓	✓			✓	✓		✓

Figure 1. Parent's record of antecedents and consequences to projectile vomiting in a medically fragile 3-year-old child. (Form 9 in Appendix.) *Comments:* The parent was instructed to record the time and number of vomiting episodes in rapid succession by placing a tally mark for each episode. Coughing and gagging were also recorded to determine if they occurred at times without subsequent vomiting. If the child vomited or gagged/coughed more than once in rapid succession, these were tallied on the same line. Based on parent report, antecedents and consequences possibly influencing the behavior were listed. When vomiting/gagging/coughing occurred, she checked all relevant boxes under "Antecedents" and "Consequences," and added anything else under "Comments." Note that, in addition to being recorded separately as a target behavior, "gag/cough" is listed as a possible antecedent to vomiting. The form is adapted from O'Neill et al. (1990), reprinted with permission from Wadsworth Publishing.

Because the therapist noted some coughing and gagging in clinic, the parent was also asked to record these behaviors using ABC recording, in order to determine if they might be involved in bringing on the vomiting. She also recorded antecedent environmental events that she and the therapist determined might be precipitating the vomiting, as well as immediate and delayed consequences occurring after the behavior. Figure 1 shows the mother's first two days of data. Based on these data, we hypothesized that these behaviors served the functions of getting attention in the form of the child's getting his clothes and canula changed, staying home with Mom, and possibly being reprimanded. They also served to avoid activities outside the home. The sight of his coat seemed to serve as a cue for the behaviors because it usually meant that the child was about to leave the home. Furthermore, gagging and coughing almost always preceded vomiting. Note, however, that receiving medication was also an antecedent, suggesting that the medication may have been upsetting his stomach and setting the stage for vomiting.

Based on such data, taken over a week, the therapist further assessed any aversive events occurring outside the home. In this case, the boy attended many school and doctor's appointments, which were aversive for both the child and his mother. The therapist also determined that the boy was less likely to vomit when his father took him out of the house, perhaps because his father only took him to pleasurable activities such as on a drive or to the zoo and not to doctor's appointments.

To complete the story, let us describe the intervention and its effects. Intervention consisted of several components: (a) the timing of medication was adjusted; (b) components of the aversive activities were changed to make them more pleasurable whenever possible; (c) fading procedures were introduced in which the child's father got him out the door and his mother then joined them for the pleasurable activities (during which he was rewarded for getting out the door without vomiting) and difficult activities were gradually faded in; (d) the parents gave a mild reprimand when the boy gagged or coughed and then praised any efforts he made to thwart vomiting; and (e) vomiting was handled in a matter-of-fact manner by quickly replacing the canula with a spare one, cleaning up excess vomit, and changing his clothes once he reached their destination (rather than at home). Within a month vomiting was limited to easily identified medical situations and he was able to leave the house consistently for any type of activity without vomiting.

O'Neill et al. (1990) also ask for "perceived functions"—that is, what the observer guesses to be the function—such as "getting attention" or "escaping an activity." A column can easily be added to our form if the clinician wishes to track perceived functions as well. Form 8 in the Appendix shows another format for collecting ABC data. This is more open-ended and narrative than the form in Figure 1. It is probably more useful when the child or parents have very little insight into the possible antecedents to or consequences of the behavior. Meyer and Janney (1989) offer yet another format.

Often the clinician will prefer to begin by finding out such things as how often, how long, or how intensely a problem behavior occurs, or perhaps how often a deficit behavior fails to occur. ABC recording of some particular behavior might be initiated later, or it may not be used at all if the clinician feels confident that he or she already has a good idea of the environmental variables influencing the behavior.

If ABC recording is not chosen as the first effort, the clinician and family should agree upon one to three behaviors on which to collect data, behaviors that seem likely to be of importance. Consider measuring an undesired child behavior, a desired child behavior, and perhaps even a desired or undesired parent behavior. This last can be measured by the very parent who is exhibiting the behavior, but it might also be measured by someone else in the home, such as a spouse, a friend, a sibling of the target child, or the child him or herself. It would be fortunate if the behaviors on which data are initially collected turned out to be ones that the clinician finds relevant throughout treatment, but that is not crucial at this point. Even if none of the data proved to be useful in themselves—which is unlikely—this initial data collection provides an assessment of the family members' motivation, organization, and ability to follow instructions, all of which will be important if subsequent treatment is to succeed. Furthermore, it sets up an expectation regarding the "homework" necessary for successful treatment. The important thing is to get the family started collecting data from the beginning.

To show that the clinician too is serious and committed to the collection and use of quantitative clinical information, he or she should have forms ready that can be easily adapted for recording a variety of data by a variety of methods. It is not wise simply to tell a parent, "When you get home, get a piece of paper and put a tally on it every time Tim does _____." The clinician's being so casual about data collection implies that it is not very important. The data collection should be treated as systematically and professionally as any other part of the clinician's services.

Making the Data-Collecting Task Realistic in Difficulty

If one is considering ABC recording, it is important to recognize that it is intense. It is not realistic to ask most parents to do such recording for every instance of a behavior that typically occurs, say, eight or more times a day. Instead, a sample can be obtained. For example, a parent could be asked how realistic it would be for them to record the first four instances each day. Since they are recording the time that the behavior occurs, this information will still provide an idea of overall frequency of the behavior. Also, if the parent is sometimes not present when the behavior occurs, he or she can just write down the time of day he or she knows it to have occurred and anything else he or she knows about the situation, leaving the rest of the form blank.

If ABC recording is not being requested, it may be reasonable to ask some-one to record all instances throughout the day. However, depending on the method of recording being used (see Chapter 3), the frequency of the behavior, the person's other responsibilities, and other factors, it still may be necessary to restrict the data collection to certain times or situations. Discuss with the person how the data collecting is likely to go, and find ways to make it realistic and yet sufficiently informative. However, remember that with less than 5 or 10 samples in a week, one's ability to analyze the factors influencing the behavior and the success of one's interventions are will be severely limited.

SELECTING TARGET BEHAVIORS OR ENVIRONMENTAL EVENTS TO MEASURE AND POTENTIALLY CHANGE

A full description of the process of selecting target behaviors and environmental events is far too complex a topic for this book (e.g., see Evans & Meyer, 1985; Hawkins, 1986). However, we can characterize the process, which we shall call "arriving at a functional formulation." This is also called "functional analysis" (e.g., Hawkins, 1986; O'Neill et al., 1990) and is a hypothesis about what is currently causing a problem. To arrive at a functional formulation or hypothesis, study the case to decide what past learning experiences and current environmental circumstances may have led to the behavioral deficits and excesses that constitute a problem. Interviews are almost universally a part of the process—perhaps supplemented with standardized and non-standardized tests, questionnaires, or checklists—but observations by the clinician, a family member, or another relevant person will often be crucial. The process should always result in a hypothesis that specifies important behaviors to change and the environmental factors that probably need to be altered in order to change those target behaviors. Usually the target behaviors are the child's while the environmental factors might include certain parent, sibling, teacher, or others' behaviors, the kind of schoolwork the child is assigned, the child's diet, where the child sleeps, or the parents' schedules. A general rule is that target behaviors should be ones that are important to the child's long-term social, personal, academic, and family functioning. Behaviors may be targeted because they are excessive in frequency, intensity, or duration; because they are deficient in one of these three dimensions; or because they are occurring under inappropriate stimulus conditions (times or places).

It is best, when selecting child behaviors as targets, if at least one of these behaviors is a desirable one, a behavior that is to be increased in frequency. This makes it more likely that there will be a focus on expanding the child's behavioral repertoire, not merely on eliminating a problem behavior (see Hawkins, 1986), and it is likely to be a more positive experience for the child. While a skillful clinician is always looking toward the long-term benefits and costs of the target behaviors, it is common for family, teachers, and staff to give major weight to short-term considerations—sometimes only their own convenience and comfort—which tends to lead to some form of punishment as the sole intervention. Therefore, the clinician may need to spend considerable time educating family, teachers, or staff about whose behaviors are really most important to change, which behaviors are most important in the long run, and why. This issue is often profoundly important. Consider the following example:

> A couple brings in their 12-year-old son who they complain "is always fighting, sullen, disobedient, sassy, and sneakily destroying property." It is tempting to directly target those specific child behaviors, since that is what the parents are complaining about. The boy may say little during the interview, so he is not offering alternatives. However, by conducting a more thorough assessment of the case, it may be discovered that: there is a younger sister who "can do no wrong" in her parents' eyes; the parents pay little attention to the boy except to punish him; they seem to be angry at him all the time, even when he has been behaving acceptably; and they exclude him from some activities due to his "bad behavior." Knowing these further facts—ones that might not be discovered without observing in the home and interviewing the boy and his sister—would suggest that designing an intervention that is focused on the boy's problem behavior alone would be inappropriate.

In this example, the most important thing to change is the environmental events that the boy experiences, particularly the *parents'* behavior. Thus, these events are also the most important to measure. The boy is probably reacting to the parents' apparent rejection, which may have begun when his sister was born and increased since then. Of course, once the parents have learned to exhibit more interest, affection, and support, there may still be child behaviors that need to be addressed directly. Having addressed the parents' behavior initially, however, makes these youth behaviors more likely to change and the improved behavior more likely to last.

Eventually the child, family, and clinician need to settle on a small number of behavioral and/or environmental events to measure consistently, especially one or more behaviors that the functional formulation suggests as crucial targets for change. If it is reasonable, also measure one or more behaviors that are not being subjected to direct intervention, such as behaviors that could change as a positive or negative side effect of the treatment. One may wish to collect only crude or occasional (e.g., once a month) information on these side effects, to save effort.

Defining and Measuring Target Behaviors

Once target behaviors—and any environmental events to be measured—have been identified for data collection, they should be defined explicitly, with the help of the child or adults involved, so the information will accurately reflect those behaviors. Each definition should be as objective as possible, referring to observable characteristics of the behavior or environment.

When defining for scientific purposes, each definition needs to be so unambiguous that anyone reading it carefully for the first time would understand well enough to be able to collect the data themselves from that written definition alone, without further training. However, such precision is not necessary for clinical use. Nevertheless, it is usually helpful to list important components of the behavior, give some typical examples, and give some questionable instances. For example, notice how different the following definitions are from one another:

Definition #1:   *Leaving a Mess*: Whenever Jerry leaves something out.

Definition #2:   *Leaving a Mess*: Whenever Jerry leaves out a plate, eating utensil, glass or cup, article of clothing, piece of paper (if larger than a thumbnail), hobby or craft item (larger than a thumbnail), or a toy or sports item for longer than 30 minutes after he has stopped using it. An exception would be when he stops for a meal or snack or to do some chore that his parents want him to do; however, when the meal or chore is finished, the 30-minute timing begins.

Each mess is counted once, regardless how many items are in it; except that if an item is separated from the other item(s) by more than 6 feet, it is considered a separate mess and also counted.

The second definition makes it much clearer when a "mess" should be recorded and how many counts should be given.

It is best to arrive at a definition through experience with the specific case. That is, write an initial definition as well as possible through discussion with the child and family, but then the clinician or other observer should try it out and improve it wherever necessary. If practical, have two people try recording the same behavior at the same time, but independently; that is, without being able to detect what the other person is recording. Such interobserver reliability checks are a good way to find the weaknesses in a definition so that it can be improved.

If the definition cannot be tried out first, be sure that the observer writes down questions and problems that come up during his or her testing of it. Then when he or she brings back the quantitative information, review the problems and questions that arose. If he or she reports that none arose, quiz him or her about the individual events he or she recorded to see what he or she decided to do in various situations. There are likely to be ways that the definition or data-recording method needs improvement. Make the improvements and have the data collector continue the recording. After that, it is still wise to discuss the specific events and improve the definition, if needed, but the information already collected is not necessarily invalid because of that. It probably is adequate for clinical purposes.

Sometimes, too, definitions need to be revised as children find loopholes or the adult recognizes a needed intervention change. For instance, in our first case study in Chapter 9, the definition of "aggression" might have needed to be changed to include hugging another child, since the adult was unable to intervene fast enough to prevent biting when the child hugged.

For some behaviors, it may be necessary to include level of intensity in the definition of the behavior. An example might be recording how often a very shy child spoke to a peer. An observer will have to decide whether "speaking" is defined as when the child moves her lips (even if neither the observer nor the peer could hear anything), when sounds can be heard (but words cannot be deciphered), or when words are understandable at 5 feet or 10 feet. Without defining "speaking" with this kind of clarity, the clinician and parents may not be able to determine the clinical significance of any behavior change. Later in this chapter, an example will be given where a definition for speaking was devised (see Figure 3).

The following are three examples of very clear operational definitions of behavior. They illustrate the kinds of information that can be helpful in clarifying what is meant by such vague terms as "aggression," "disruptive," "selfish," "conversation," or "helpful." Remember, it is best to make individualized definitions and to make sure that all observers understand and are in agreement with the definition. For more on defining behavior, especially for scientific purposes, see Hawkins and Dobes (1977).

AGGRESSION is whenever Benjie does something intended to hurt another person, hurt their feelings, interfere with their activities, or destroy property valuable to someone, even to himself.

Examples: throwing a stick at someone, hitting or trying to hit someone with his fist, calling another child a bad name, teasing another child, tipping over another child's toys, standing in front of the slide so no one can come down safely, tearing up his own picture.

Non-examples: yelling loudly (if not calling someone a name or teasing), swinging his arms around but not at or near someone, stomping away in anger, breaking a stick (unless that was someone's plaything).

HELPING MOTHER means doing something that pleases Mother by reducing her workload (or is intended to do so at least) or making a situation more enjoyable for her.

Examples: clearing dirty dishes from the table, raking leaves and putting them in a leaf bag, asking if Mother would like the paper to read, carrying in groceries.

Non-examples: stopping or avoiding some annoying behavior he's doing or has done in the past, doing one of his regular chores, cleaning up his own clothes or playthings, offering to help but not with something Mother really wants help with.

POSITIVE TALK means any talk about anyone or anything that is cheerful, optimistic, upbeat, complimentary, affectionate, supportive of someone, or such. The person or thing being spoken of need not be present.

Examples: "I'm a great soccer player." "I like blue, it's my favorite color." "She couldn't help it; the bus was late." "It's really hard, isn't it?" (when someone is having difficulty with a task). "I'm going to take this flower to my teacher." "That's a cool shirt." "I liked that book" (even though it is complimentary of a thing, rather than a person).

Non-examples: "Fine" (when just a perfunctory answer to "How are you?") "Are you going to play?" (when it is not clearly an invitation to play). "Would you give me a hand?" (when it is not clear that this fits the definition).

DECIDE HOW TO MEASURE THE BEHAVIOR AND/OR ENVIRONMENTAL EVENTS

Once behaviors have been targeted and defined, the next step is to select a measurement method that fits the behavior, environment, and purpose. Several direct measurement methods are available: frequency, duration, latency, interval recording, momentary time sampling, quality recording, task achievement recording, and cue-effectiveness recording. This book will present these as different record-

Table 1.1. Types of Measurement Methods, Appropriate Applications, and Examples

	Description	When to use	When *not* to use	Examples
Frequency	Records how often the behavior occurs	For discrete behavior that's to be increased or decreased in frequency	When rate is too fast (e.g., number words spoken) or accuracy or duration important	• Initiating conversation • Aggression • Pestering
Duration	Records how long the behavior lasts each time	For continuous behavior, where percent time engaged in it is important	When behavior is discrete and of brief duration	• Thumbsucking • Time taken to eat meal • Length of nap
Latency	Records how long until a behavior occurs after the cue for it	When time between cue and response is of interest, speed of reacting	When frequency, duration, quality, or regularity is really the interest	• Time to fall asleep • Time to come to dinner when called • Time to start homework after timer goes off
Interval recording	Records whether or not the behavior occurred within each preset interval	When observation time is limited or when recording several behaviors	When accurate frequency, duration, quality, or regularity is really the interest	• Playing cooperatively • Interacting with others • One or more problem behaviors from a list
Momentary time sampling	Records whether the behavior is ongoing at preset moments; low-cost measure of duration	When observation time is very limited or observation needs to be unobtrusive	When behavior is brief or infrequent; when frequency, quality, or regularity is really the interest	• Watching TV • On-task behavior in school • Cooperative vs. isolated play • Conversing
Quality recording	Records how well the behavior is performed, according to criteria specified	When "how it is done" (accuracy/topography) is primary interest	When frequency, duration, or regularity is the interest	• Checklist of a clean room, mowed lawn, cleared table, etc.

	Records	When	Examples
Task achievement	Records when each of a series of tasks/skills is achieved at criterion level	When documenting progress through a series of skills/tasks to be mastered	• Achieving self-help skill • Reading new words • Approaching series of feared situations
Cue-effectiveness	Records whether the behavior occurs each time a cue for it occurs	When determining whether the behavior is under desired stimulus control	• Percent of parent commands/requests complied with • Saying "Thank you" at appropriate time • Brings assignments home
Checklist	Records if an event occurred (e.g., each day) or characteristic is shown	When time is limited and answers are clear "yes" or "no"	• Completion of homework • Completion of chores • School misbehaviors
Rating scale	Records the intensity of behavior as judged subjectively	When objective measurement is not possible and intensity is the interest	• Pain intensity • SUDS rating of anxiety/fear • Loudness of speech

(Additional "When" examples noted in table:) When determining frequency, duration, or quality of performance of an existing skill — When many different, vague, or subtle cues might evoke the behavior, so one can't readily tell when it "should" occur — When actual frequency, duration, etc., is easy enough to record — When objective data can be obtained instead

ing methods, although some of them actually overlap. A summary of these different methods, when they are most applicable, and an example of each, may be found in Table 1, which includes eight methods that will be discussed in this chapter and two that will be discussed in Chapter 4.

Frequency

The simplest method for collecting quantitative information is often a frequency count, in which each occurrence of the target response is recorded. A frequency count is appropriate when the target behavior is discrete and the initiation and termination of the behavior are clear, so that separate occurrences can be easily discriminated. Also, the rate of responding must not be too fast to count. For example, the speed of speech usually precludes counting the number of words a person speaks (unless tape recorded and analyzed carefully after the fact, which would rarely be relevant in clinical services).

When measuring a behavior, the opportunities for the behavior need to remain fairly constant, otherwise the data may reflect only changes in the opportunities provided by the environment, not changes in the behavior. In order to keep opportunities for responding reasonably constant, the data collector should either observe for a fixed length of time each day or measure the length of time he or she does observe. Then the rate of response during each such session can be calculated by dividing the frequency by the number of minutes of observation. This yields "frequency per minute" (rate) so that comparisons can be made between unequal time periods. Of course, the rate will often be tiny, such as .0001 per minute, so it may be appropriate to multiply it by 60 so that it will be a larger number and rate per hour. It could even be multiplied by 600 to yield rate per 10 hours, if the client finds that easier to understand.

Frequency counts are probably most often kept by putting tallies on a sheet of paper, but they may also be recorded on golfers' wrist counters or pocket counters such as those used in keeping track of grocery purchases (1 cent representing 1 response). A particularly unobtrusive method of recording, if unobtrusiveness is important, is to shift a coin from one pants pocket to another each time the response occurs. Another is to make a tally mark on the inside of one's wrist with each occurrence, or on a piece of tape stuck on the wrist.

Examples of behaviors for which frequency counts could be used include leaving a mess, hitting another person or object, initiating a conversation, or sharing with others. When attempting to measure an event that actually contains a series of individual responses—such as "fighting with brother" or "swearing"—it often helps to call it an "episode of fighting" or "episode of swearing," so that each single fighting response or each swear word need not be tallied. However, the definition needs to include a specification of what length of pause (or other event) between the events constitutes the end of one episode. That is, there needs to be an objective cri-

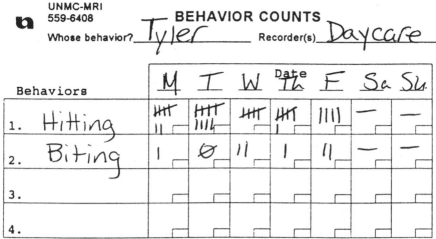

Figure 2. Frequency of aggression in a 3-year-old girl: Biting and hitting in daycare, recorded by the daycare teacher for 1 week on an index. (Form 10 in Appendix.) *Comments:* The daycare teacher was asked to make tally marks each time Tyler was aggressive toward an adult or child. The index card was used for portability in the classroom and on the playground.

terion by which the observer will decide that a fight or conversation has ended and that any further fighting responses or swearing constitute a new episode.

Figure 2 gives an example involving a 3-year-old boy who, because of aggression toward his peers, was in danger of being expelled from his daycare. Using an index card, the teacher was asked simply to make a tally mark each time the child exhibited aggressive behavior (broken down into hitting and biting, the two types of aggression that were problematic). The parents also saw aggression at home and were recording this separately.

Another, more complicated, example of frequency recording is depicted in Figure 3. This case was a girl with selective mutism. Home observations of nonverbal gestures, words, and longer exchanges were recorded. The mother was asked to select 5-minute samples throughout the day in which the child had contact with "familiar" (F) and "unfamiliar" (U) people and in locations of varying difficulty (e.g., home, at dance class, at a store). By our definition, "familiar" people were those with whom she spoke regularly and without hesitation before treatment. At the outset of treatment, the mother provided us with a complete list of "familiar" people. All others were considered "unfamiliar," even if she knew them well (as was the case with one aunt) and even after she began to speak with them. The girl was then asked to rate her level of anxiety on a 5-point scale (Subjective Units of Discomfort or "SUDS" rating).

NAME: Kelsea   MONTH: June   OBSERVER: Mom
BEHAVIOR(S): 5-minute samples of talking
INSTRUCTIONS: Record non-verbal only if there are no verbals

DATE	Location	Person	U/F	Non-Verbal	Verbal	SUDS(1-5)	COMMENTS
6/20	Grammy's	Grammy	F	—	25	1	
"	store	Mom	F	—	11	3	Clinging to Mom
"	Dentist	Dentist	U	∅	∅	5	

Nonverbal   = *Gestures or whispers* (cannot decipher words)
Verbal   = *Audible at 5 feet*
                     Record single words with tally marks
                     Record multiword utterances with *one* tally mark
                     (one utterance ends when another person speaks or 5 seconds of silence
                     elapse)
Familiar (F)   = *Anyone Kelsea spoke with regularly before we began seeing her (from list)*
Unfamiliar (U)   = *Anyone else*
SUDS   1------------2------------3------------4-----------5
                     Not anxious   Very anxious

Figure 3. Frequency of nonverbal and verbal exchanges in a girl with selective mutism, recorded by the mother. (Adaptation of Form 1 in Appendix.) *Comments:* The mother recorded 5-minute samples throughout the day in which the child had contact with "familiar" (F) and "unfamiliar" (U) people and in locations of varying difficulty (e.g., home, at dance class, at a store). "Familiar" people were defined as those with whom she spoke regularly and without hesitation before treatment. All others were defined as "Unfamiliar." Nonverbal interactions were not recorded if she verbalized. After the 5-minute sample the child was asked to rate her anxiety (SUDS) on a 5-point scale. The exchanges were tallied by the mother on a separate sheet, then transferred to this form.

By mutual agreement with the mother, operational definitions were developed for nonverbal gestures ("nonverbal"), and for "verbalizations" (single spoken words and phrases of two or more words that were understood at 5 feet or more). These definitions were typed at the bottom of the recording sheet to ensure reliability. The verbal phrases, while counted the same as single words, were defined so that, when the child was speaking fluently, the parent would not be expected to record individual words in rapid speech (as discussed previously in this chapter). Figure 4 presents a summary of the clinical information collected on this girl's interactions at home and in the clinic.

Duration

Duration refers to how long a person engages in the target behavior and is measured by such methods as starting a stopwatch at response onset and stopping it at response offset. The length of time that the behavior occurred is then written down and the stopwatch is usually reset to zero and re-started when the behavior begins

NAME: Kelsea   MONTH: June   OBSERVER: Mom, Therapist

BEHAVIOR(S): 5-minute samples of talking across people and locations. "Familiar" = person Kelsea talked to freely in baseline. "Unfamiliar" = all other people.

DATE	HOME: Familiar		HOME: Unfamiliar			CLINIC			COMMENTS
	Non-Verbal	Verbal	Non-Verbal	Verbal	Person	Non-Verbal	Verbal	Person	
6-19	—	16							BASELINE
"									=
6-20	—	25							BASELINE
"			1	Ø	Freeman				=
"			Ø	Ø	Dentist				=
"	—	11				Ø	Ø	JRM	mother present in room
									=

Figure 4. Summary of nonverbal and verbal exchanges in a girl with selective mutism, recorded by the parent and therapist (Form 4 in Appendix.) *Comments:* The therapist consolidated all clinical information from home and clinic. Home data were collapsed into the presence of "Familiar" and "Unfamiliar" people, and the "Unfamiliar" person was listed. In the clinic data, "Person" referred to the individual who initiates the interaction. Under "Comments," the phase of intervention was noted. Each 5-minute sample was listed on a separate line, and a horizontal line was drawn through a block if the behavior was not observed.

again. An alternative is to record the cumulative time by not resetting the watch after an episode of the behavior, but information on the frequency of episodes is then lost.

Behaviors whose duration might be of interest are tantrums, the percentage of time spent thumb-sucking, or time spent working on homework. Notice that duration can be used as a measure of how efficient a person is becoming, such as measuring how long it takes a youngster to complete her homework each evening or to clean up her room. Of course, it would also be necessary to assure that the task was actually completed, in terms of some explicit criteria. Similarly, one could measure how long it takes a youngster to get ready for school in the morning, which means the time between his or her being called and being at the door, properly toileted, dressed, and fed. This could also be called the latency of the child's getting those tasks done, and latency recording will be described shortly.

A stopwatch is the most precise way to measure response duration, and some wristwatches have a stopwatch with an elapsed time indicator. Using a clock or watch is usually too crude unless the behavior is one that usually occurs only in long episodes, such as watching TV or mowing the lawn. If using a clock be sure the parent or adolescent writes down the time when the behavior started ("start time") and the time when it ended ("stop time"), and be sure to define what constitutes the starting and stopping of the behavior.

One issue that may need to be decided is how to treat brief pauses in the behavior. For example, if a 10-year-old were recording how long she plays with her little brother, what happens when there is a pause to go to the bathroom or get a drink? The clinician could specify that any pause of less than 7 minutes is not subtracted from the total duration unless there is a second pause during the same episode. On the other hand, if a parent is recording how long the child practices a musical instrument, all pauses (or all pauses of more than 1 minute) should probably be subtracted from the total. These examples demonstrate how carefully the clinician must attend to details (and make individual decisions) in recording so that the observations provide an accurate picture.

Another issue to consider is activity level. If a teacher were recording a withdrawn child's playing with peers, would it be sufficient that the child is merely within certain distance of the peers and watching them? Or must there be some kind of two-way interaction? If the latter, what constitutes "two-way"?

Figures 5 and 6 present an example of a mother's recording of the duration of her 2-year-old's wearing glasses, and a summary graph. This child was visually and hearing impaired and refused to wear both his glasses and his hearing aids, resulting in his receiving very poor sensory input from the environment. Glasses-wearing was first taught through a reinforcement and fading procedure, in which acceptance of the glasses nearer and nearer to his face was reinforced. Once he accepted them on his face, the duration of this acceptance was targeted. The mother used a stopwatch and recorded the total length of time the child kept his glasses on. Because

NAME: Mark   MONTH: Dec/Jan   OBSERVER: Mom

BEHAVIOR(S): # minute's wearing glasses

DATE	Time: Start	Time: End	TOTAL TIME ON	# times tried to take off	COMMENTS
12/12	3:42 pm	4:42	60'	0	In Car
12/19	2:01 pm	3:41	100'	2	Interactive Game
1/5	10:5 am	11:52	53'	4	Interactive Game

Figure 5. Duration of glasses-wearing in a 2-year-old with aphakia (lens removed from eye). (Adaptation of Form 1 in Appendix.) *Comments:* The mother kept track of the total time Mark wore his glasses and the number of times he tried to take them off. Note that she has recorded start and finish time, then subtracted to determine the total time. She also noted the activity on occasion.

she was instructed to replace the glasses immediately when he removed them, she did not subtract for pauses, but instead simply recorded the frequency of that behavior as well. The summary graph helped the mother to see *visually* the progress she was making in improving the child's compliance with glasses-wearing.

One difficulty with measuring response duration is that it often requires almost continuous attention from the observer during the observation period. Due to this limitation, clinicians only measure duration if length of responding is a high priority. When duration is too demanding to measure, clinicians should consider using momentary time sampling—to be described later—which is a good index of duration and usually easier to apply. Even interval recording, also described later, might be useful.

Latency

Latency is similar to duration in that it requires a measure of time, but instead of recording the length of responding, the observer records the time between the occurrence of a specific stimulus or cue and the onset of the target behavior. An example of this would be the time it takes for a child to begin complying (the target behavior) with a parental request (the environmental cue). Other examples would be the number of minutes it takes to fall asleep after going to bed or the time it takes a child to get out of bed when called.

Figures 7 and 8 are samples of data collected on a 14-year-old boy who developed a phobia of swallowing following a choking episode. He had lost 50 pounds in a 3-month period and was only eating soft foods. A swallowing study, using video flouroscopy, revealed that all swallowing mechanisms were intact, but he was chewing the food excessively, bringing the bolus of food to the back of his

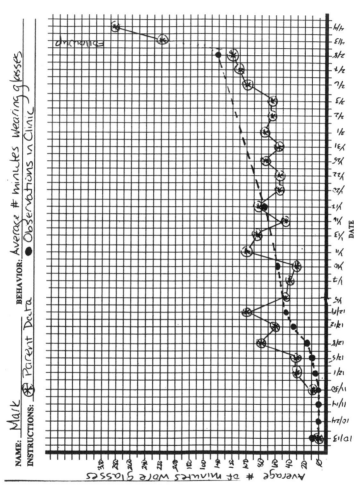

Figure 6. Graph of average duration of wearing glasses in a 2-year-old with aphakia (lens removed from eye). (Form 7 in Appendix). *Comments:* Parent data and clinic data were graphed separately. The clinic observations paralleled the mother's home observations, suggesting that she was an accurate observer. Drops in the duration usually occurred at times when Mark was sick or the parent had a busy schedule and took his glasses off early.

NAME: Deon MONTH: March OBSERVER: ALR

BEHAVIOR(S): Swallowing - Clinic Observations

DATE	FOOD	# sec. to swallow	# swallows saliva	x̄ EMG	Clinician EMG	SUDS (1-5)	COMMENTS
3/5	Drink	1"	0	4.1	x̄ = 5.7	1	
		1"	0				
	Banana	7"	0	18.2	x̄ = 7.1	2	
		7"	0			2	
		11"	0			2	
	Cookie	7"	0	15.7	x̄ = 7.9	3	
		10"	0			2	
3/21	Sausage	½"	1	19.3	x̄ = 7.8	4	
		½"	0			4	
		½"	0			4	
		¾"	2			5	
		1"	3			5	
		1¼"	2			5	
		½"	1			4	
3/5	Apple	8	0	18.6	x̄ = 10.1	3	
		12	0			3	
		12	0			3	
TOTAL							

Figure 7. Clinic observations of swallowing in a 14-year-old boy with a swallowing phobia following a choking episode. (Adaptation of Form 4 in Appendix.) *Comments:* The clinician presented the adolescent with foods of varying textures and recorded the latency (in seconds) to swallow, the frequency of swallows of saliva (without swallowing the bolus of food), and his SUDS (1–5) rating of anxiety. Because it was hypothesized that muscle tension might make swallowing difficult, mean EMG readings (calculated automatically by the computer) were taken during baseline. A clinician served as a comparison, since no normative data on muscle tension during swallowing were available.

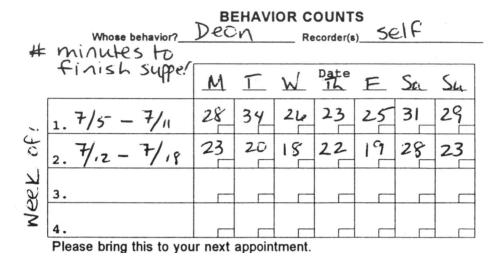

BEHAVIOR COUNTS

Whose behavior? _Deon_   Recorder(s) _self_

\# minutes to finish supper!

Week of:

	Date M	T	W	Th	F	Sa	Su
1. 7/5 – 7/11	28	34	26	23	25	31	29
2. 7/12 – 7/18	23	20	18	22	19	28	23
3.							
4.							

Please bring this to your next appointment.

Figure 8. Duration of meals in a 14-year-old boy with a swallowing phobia. (Form 10 in Appendix.) *Comments:* The adolescent himself timed the length of the meal, using a stopwatch. The second week is the beginning of intervention.

mouth, readying himself to swallow, then pushing the food forward again and repeating the above process several times before eventually swallowing the bolus, which had become almost liquid. Based on this observation, it was hypothesized that there was excessive muscle tension when swallowing, making it difficult to pass the bolus down the esophagus.

To test this hypothesis in clinic, EMG readings of throat tension in this young man were taken while he was eating a variety of foods of increasingly difficult textures (e.g., macaroni, apple, hamburger, carrot). Similar EMG readings were obtained in another young adult for comparison purposes. In addition, information was obtained on the latency in seconds of his swallowing bites of food, as well as the number of swallows of saliva while chewing. He was also asked to give a SUDS rating of anxiety after swallowing each type of food. The client data are depicted in Figure 7. When interviewed, his mother reported that at home he chewed his food excessively before swallowing, resulting in very long meals. Consequently, the primary information, recorded at home by the boy, was the number of minutes to complete his meal, which is depicted in Figure 8.

Interval Recording

Interval recording is a type of noncontinuous recording that combines aspects of both frequency and duration recording. A block of time—a day, an evening, a selected hour of the day, etc.—is first divided into equal intervals (e.g., 15 sec., 1 min., 10 min., 1 hr., one-third day) and the target behavior is recorded as present or absent for each interval. That is, the observer records "yes" if the behavior is occurring at *any* time during the interval and "no" if it never occurs during the interval. Once "yes"—or a simple symbol to denote "yes"—is recorded for an interval, it is no longer necessary to observe for the remainder of that interval, thus greatly decreasing the continuous observation time for the data collector. The observations can then be graphed as a percentage: the number of intervals in which the target behavior occurred divided by the total number of intervals in which it could have occurred (the number of intervals of recording).

An interesting form of interval recording is the Parent Daily Report developed by Patterson, Reid, Jones, and Conger (1975; see also Chamberlain & Reid, 1987). Each day a secretary or other clinic staff interviews the parent briefly by phone at an agreed-upon time, going through a list of problem child behaviors (though it would be good to also include desirable behaviors) that are at least tentative targets for that individual child (and/or parent, sibling, etc.). The parent has copies of the same list at home and has marked information on that day's copy. The interviewer's task is to find out which of those behaviors, if any, occurred during that day and, if any did, in what setting. Notice that this method treats a whole day as an interval. While this may be a crude datum for most scientific purposes, it can be quite adequate for clinical purposes, and it is *far* better than merely asking the parent to recall events when the parent is in the clinic once a week.

One variant of interval recording is spaced-interval recording, which involves the same procedure as interval recording, except that nonobserving intervals are placed between observing intervals. This is used to give the observer time to record what he or she just observed, time to observe a different person's behavior, time to observe some other behavior, or time to carry out other tasks unrelated to the behavior. Since intervals can be spaced throughout the day, rather than concentrated in one time block, this can give a more comprehensive assessment of a target behavior.

Another variation of interval recording is a scatterplot. Figure 9 depicts a scatterplot (adapted from Touchette, MacDonald, & Langer, 1985), in which the parent noted whether the child sucked his thumb continually during an interval (solid block), during part of the interval (diagonal line through block), or not at all during the interval (no mark in the block). No opportunity to observe the behavior is denoted by a vertical line through the block. This format is particularly helpful when it would be too difficult for the child or family to count or time every instance of a behavior. Although not as accurate as timing the duration, it gives a global picture, not only of frequency and duration, but also of possible patterns across the day, which can reveal something about causal factors.

Figure 10 depicts another example of interval recording used in one clinic with young children being assessed for autism. Because children with autism have

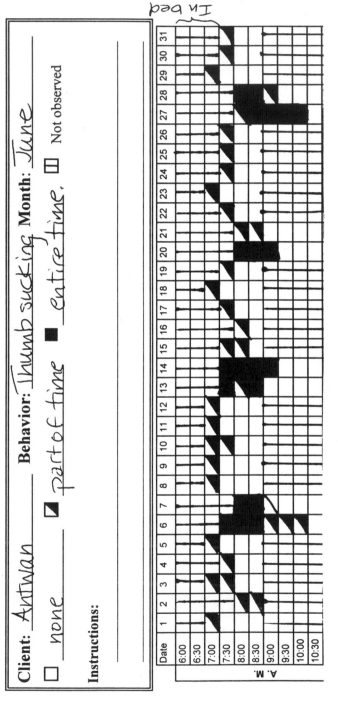

Figure 9. Interval recording of thumbsucking, using a scatterplot. (Form 20 in Appendix.) *Comments:* A scatterplot was chosen to determine when the thumbsucking occurred most often during the day. Instead of the more time-consuming process of timing the duration of thumbsucking throughout the day, the parent was asked to estimate duration in half-hour intervals. This form is adapted from Touchette, MacDonald, and Langer (1985).

Child __Raoul_____ Date __Feb. 13___ Coder __SRQ_____

Adult: __Dad__ Parent _____ Clinician

PARENT-CHILD INTERACTIONS (15-SECOND INTERVALS)

IGNORE (Adult reads, child plays alone)

INTERVAL	1	2	3	4	5	6	7	8	9	10	11	12	13	14	15	16	17	18	19	20
Initiates interaction					✓						✓									
Maintains interaction																				
Constructive play (X = Activity Change)	✓	✓	✓	✓	✓									X		✓	✓	✓	✓	✓
Pretend play (X = Activity Change)						X	✓	✓	✓	✓	✓	✓	✓							
Self-injurious																				
Aggression / tantrum																				
Repetitive motor behavior																				
Repetitive pattern interest																				
Parts of objects																				

PARALLEL PLAY (Adult plays beside child with minimal interaction)

INTERVAL	1	2	3	4	5	6	7	8	9	10	11	12	13	14	15	16	17	18	19	20
Initiates interaction	✓							✓												
Maintains interaction		✓																		
Constructive play (X = Activity Change)			✓	✓	✓	✓			✓	✓	✓	X	✓	✓						
Pretend play (X = Activity Change)																X	✓	✓	✓	✓
Self-injurious																				
Aggression / tantrum																				
Repetitive motor behavior																				
Repetitive pattern interest																				
Parts of objects																				

PLAY INVITINGLY (Adult plays with another adult, minimal interaction with child)

INTERVAL	1	2	3	4	5	6	7	8	9	10	11	12	13	14	15	16	17	18	19	20
Initiates interaction	✓					✓								✓						
Maintains interaction																				
Constructive play (X = Activity Change)			✓	✓	✓															
Pretend play (X = Activity Change)																				
Self-injurious																				
Aggression (tantrum) + crying								✓	✓	✓	✓	✓	✓	✓		✓	✓		✓	✓
Repetitive motor behavior																				
Repetitive pattern interest																				
Parts of objects																				

ATTEMPT TO ENGAGE (Adult plays directly with child)

INTERVAL	1	2	3	4	5	6	7	8	9	10	11	12	13	14	15	16	17	18	19	20
Initiates interaction						✓														
Maintains interaction	✓	✓	✓	✓	✓				✓	✓	✓	✓	✓	✓	✓	✓	✓	✓	✓	✓
Constructive play (X = Activity Change)	✓	✓	✓	✓	✓	✓		X	✓	✓	✓	✓	✓	✓	✓	✓	✓	✓	✓	✓
Pretend play (X = Activity Change)																				
Self-injurious																				
Aggression / tantrum																				
Repetitive motor behavior																				
Repetitive pattern interest																				
Parts of objects																				

Figure 10. Interval recording of child behaviors across changes in adult interactions. (Adaptation of Form 15 in Appendix). *Comments:* This form is used in one clinic for recording parent–child interactions in young children being assessed for autism. The observer checks the occurrence of any of the nine child behaviors (operationally defined elsewhere) in 15-second intervals. The conditions represent changes in the amount of *adult* initiated interactions with the child. Activity changes are denoted by a "✓" in the play rows. Intervals with none of the behaviors are marked by a line through the interval number. Behaviors were collapsed into "Interaction" (Lines 1 and 2), "Play" (Lines 3 and 4), "Inappropriate Behavior" (Lines 5 and 6), and "Stereotypic Behavior" (Lines 7, 8, and 9). Data are then calculated as percent of intervals in which each of these four categories of behavior occurred.

difficulties with socialization, communication, and play skills to varying degrees, this form was developed in order to look for these characteristics (as well as inappropriate behavior). The occurrence of each of nine behaviors is recorded in 15-second intervals across each of four conditions with increasing levels of adult interaction with the child. Notice that this is a more intensive and systematic data collection procedure than we would expect of most families.

The categories of adult interactions were selected based on the hypothesis that children with autism might respond with more negative behavior when the adult attempted to engage them and to have more stereotypic behavior when left to themselves. Although normative data have not been collected on this measure, it is likely that a child *without* autism would engage in initiating adult interactions in the first three conditions and show fewer inappropriate behaviors when the adult played directly with them. Child behaviors being observed include types of play, interactions with adults, stereotypies, and negative behaviors.

In the first condition, the parent is asked to set the child up with interesting toys and then to fill out paperwork, while minimizing interactions with the child. In the second condition, the parent is asked to parallel play in close proximity to the child, again while minimizing interactions with the child. In the third condition, the parent is asked to play "enthusiastically" with another adult while minimizing interactions with the child. Finally, in the fourth condition, the parent is asked to play directly with the child. After the data were collected, behaviors were collapsed into "Interaction" (Lines 1 and 2), "Play" (Lines 3 and 4), "Inappropriate Behavior" (Lines 5 and 6), and "Stereotypic Behavior" (Lines 7, 8, and 9). Then the percent of intervals in which each of these four categories of behavior occurred was calculated.

A major advantage of interval recording is that it is flexible enough to be used with almost any behavior. It is especially useful for responses that are not discrete movements but rather states of "engagement," such as a child's remaining in his seat at school, working on homework, talking with someone, whining, playing in a certain area, or playing cooperatively. The observer needs only to decide whether or not the behavior was occurring at any time during the interval. It is not necessary to determine when the behavior began or ended, and brief pauses in the behavior are not an issue. Due to this flexibility, interval recording is useful in recording a variety of behaviors.

Interval recording reflects neither the rate (frequency per minute, hour, or day) nor the duration of the behavior with fidelity; thus, some researchers have criticized it. However, this limitation is also an advantage, because interval data reflect a combination of rate and duration and can be thought of as indicating "the amount of the behavior" very well (Baer & Fowler, 1984). If it is important that the interval data reflect rate fairly accurately, the intervals should be small enough that it would be unusual for two occurrences to happen in the same interval, yet large enough that one occurrence is unlikely to cross several intervals.

Momentary Time Sampling

Another method that reflects both frequency and duration, but especially duration, is momentary time sampling. This method is similar to interval recording, but the interval is only a split second in time. At each of several predetermined moments, the observer records whether the behavior is "present" or "absent" at the moment. These "spot checks" are cued by a timer, watch, or a signal on audiotape and the time between them may be fixed or variable.

Momentary time sampling resembles taking a series of still photographs and looking at each one to see whether a particular behavior is occurring in the photo. In contrast, frequency and duration recording resemble taking a continuous motion picture and inspecting it to observe all response onsets and offsets. Interval recording would resemble cutting the movie into segments and then inspecting each of the segments to see if the behavior was present in any of the individual frames comprising the segment.

One advantage of momentary time sampling is that it totally frees the observer between samples, so that he or she needs to spend very little time observing. Another is that the observation can be very unobtrusive, since the samples can be minutes or hours apart and can even be randomly timed. Of course, the less frequent the samples, the less representative they will be, so usually more than three or four observations per day are desirable.

Momentary time sampling is not appropriate for very short duration or infrequent behaviors (e.g., joking, fire-setting, stealing, starting fights), because the observer would often miss all occurrences of the response even though the response occurred several times. Thus, the clinical information could be very unrepresentative of real performance. On the other hand, momentary time sampling is especially appropriate when measuring engagement in an activity, such as playing with others, working, reading, watching TV, etc.

Figure 11 shows use of momentary time sampling to check on whether a child is working on homework at home. The parent was asked to check quietly at semi-random minute intervals, and record whether the child was doing homework. Figure 12 shows a similar procedure for recording on-task behavior in a school setting. In this instance, the observer records at regular 20-minute intervals whether the child is on task at that given moment. The randomness of the first example is more realistic in a home setting and keeps the child from figuring out a set time to get back on task momentarily.

It is best not to set things up so that the observer gets to decide, on the spot, just when to sample the behavior. The observer's decision to sample may be influenced by what behavior is occurring at that moment and consequently the information may be biased by the observer's motivation. For example, suppose that one target behavior was a girl's practicing her French horn. The problem was that she dawdled in getting started, wasted lots of time during the practice, and sometimes

Name: _PAOLD_   Behavior: _ON-TASK_

Instructions: _Set timer to ring at intervals, check to see if P. is on-task._

Check Your Child's Homework on Minute #:

Date:	4	4	3	5	7	9	8	8	5	6	9	9	10	6	6	7	6	8	8	9
Apr. 4	+	+	O	+	+	+	+	/ Homework done												
Apr. 5	O	O	+	O	O	T	O	O	O	+	+	O	/ Homework done							
Apr. 6.	+	+	r	+	O	O	O	+	U	+	O	O	O	+	/ Done					

Figure 11. Momentary time sampling of on-task behavior during homework time, with variable intervals. (Adaptation of Form 19 in Appendix.) *Comments:* The parent was asked to check quitely and semi-randomly, at predetermined times (e.g., "minute #4") and record whether the child was doing homework at the moment.

quit early. Her father was taking momentary time samples during her afternoon practice times, getting about ten samples in an hour's practice time. The father was sampling merely whether she was making a sound on the French horn at the moment of each sample. However, if the timing of the samples was not prearranged, the father might unintentionally select moments to sample the behavior based on his own mood (e.g., when irritated, he might take samples when she is not producing sounds) or on his desire to prove a point or to be "fair" (e.g, if he wanted to focus on the positive, he might do just the opposite).

This problem will exist any time the observer is asked to keep track of the time on his or her watch, because he or she will be more likely even to *look* at his or her watch when the child is engaging in the inappropriate target behavior. The solution in the case of the horn player is to have the father use a simple timer (electronic or mechanical), set it for perhaps 6 minutes at the beginning of the girl's

Name: _PAOLD_   Date: _APRIL 5_

Instructions: _Check off if the child is doing the behavior AT THE MOMENT_

Interval Length: _20 minutes._

		math			reading			library	lunch	reading										
Behavior	1	2	3	4	5	6	7	8	9	10	11	12	13	14	15	16	17	18	19	20
ON-TASK	+	O	O	+	NA	O	O	+	O	O	O	U	NA	NA	+	+	+	O		
HANDS TO SELF	+	+	O	+	+	+	+	+	O	O	+	O	+	O	+	+	O	O		

Figure 12. Momentary time sampling of on-task behavior in school, with fixed intervals between samples. (Adaptation of Form 19 in Appendix.) *Comments:* This is a similar procedure to that in Figure 11. Instead of variable, the intervals were fixed, making the observations more feasible for a teacher. The teacher use a timer on her watch to cue her to observe and record.

practice time, record the state of the girl's behavior at the moment when the timer goes off, then reset the timer for another 6 minutes. Another solution might be to make up a few cards with random times on them for the timer to go off and ask the father to shuffle them daily and use whichever one comes out on top. This is the method used by the mother who recorded the data in Figure 11.

Another way for an observer to signal him or herself is to record signals on an audiotape and play it during the times when he or she is to observe. In the above example, the clinician could make a tape of randomly spaced tones. Then the father could just play that tape for himself during horn practice time, taking a sample whenever he heard the timer's signal.

The clinician may prefer to arrange it so that the girl cannot hear the timer go off, so her behavior will not be affected by the father's data-collecting. In this case, the father could use headphones. However, the timer could be used as part of the treatment, letting its sound be audible to the child and perhaps having the father give the girl a certain number of points each time she is practicing when the timer goes off, then exchanging those points for certain privileges or other rewards.

Quality Recording

Quality recording is usually used when there is a strong interest in *how* a behavior is shown—the precise form, topography, or timing of a target response. The emphasis is on the accuracy or correctness of the behavior rather than (or in addition to) the quantity of the behavior. This method involves developing a task analysis or step-by-step description (or visual model, such as a videotape or photos) of accurate performance of the target behavior and then, when observing, specifying with a check mark whether each step in the analysis was performed. For example, if the clinician were interested in how well a parent and child engage in cooperative problem-solving, all the essential steps of such problem-solving could be listed and, while the parent and child interact, each step that is completed could be checked off. To make the assessment even more detailed, the quality with which each of the steps was performed could also be subjectively rated (e.g., a Likert rating of "sincerity" or "pleasantness" of a communication).

In the earlier-mentioned case of the girl with selective mutism, the therapist reached a point where volume became a targeted outcome. To increase volume, the mother stood increasing distances away from the child and repeated what the child said. The child, Kelsea, met criteria when her response could be heard at these targeted distances. Volume was recorded as the number of feet away at which her speech could be understood (Figure 13).

Instead of recording the behaviors while they occur, they could be videotaped and then observed closely and recorded on paper afterward. The child and family can be involved in this process,. It is likely to be most useful if the observations from the videotape are done by the family and therapist together as a method

NAME: Kelsea   MONTH: _____   OBSERVER: JDN

BEHAVIOR(S): 5-minute intervals: % Audible Responses at Varying distances

⊕ Audible ⊖ Not-Audible

DATE	Location	Person	W/F	Others Present	W/F	Distance (feet)	VERBAL +	VERBAL −	% Audible	COMMENTS
6/27	Clinic	Sarah	U	Mom	F	5	HHT I	III	66%	
"	"	"	"	"	"	"	HHT III	II	80%	
"	"	"	"	"	"	"	HHT HHT	I	91%	
"	"	"	"	"	"	8	HHT III	I	89%	
"	"	"	"	"	"	10	HHT HHT I	I	92%	
6/30	Clinic	Sarah	U	Alone	−	8	HHT III	II	80%	
"	"	"	"	"	"	8	HHT I	O	100%	
"	"	"	"	"	"	10	HHT I	I	86%	

Figure 13. Intensity of voice volume in a girl with selective mutism, recorded in clinic by the therapist. (Adaptation of Form 4 in Appendix.) *Comments:* This is an extension of the case depicted in Figures 3 and 4. The target here was voice volume, recorded as the number of feet away at which her speech could be understood ("audible"). The therapist recorded the location, the person speaking directly to the child, whether that person was "familiar" by the definition given in Figure 3, and any other persons present (and whether "familiar"). The therapist then recorded the distance the mother stood from the child and whether the mother could repeat the child's verbalization accurately ("audible" vs. "inaudible"). The percent of audible responses was calculated, with a target of 85% needed before changing the distance.

of providing precise feedback. This way the child and family can learn exactly what behavior the clinician is trying to develop (or reduce) and at exactly what moments it is appropriate (or inappropriate). Using such videotapes is especially likely to be needed when the behaviors of interest occur very briefly, when there is a quick succession of such behaviors, or when the events (cues) that make a behavior appropriate (or inappropriate) are fleeting and subtle.

It is often possible to record quality from a product of the behavior rather than be concerned about the exact topography. For example, when assessing how well someone has made a bed, the exact movements that produce the result are usually of less interest than the result itself. Similarly, the quality of such behaviors as room-cleaning, dishwashing, calculating, and lawnmowing can be measured by looking at the product of the behavior.

Figure 14 depicts a very simple and crude quality rating form. The parents came to clinic complaining that their 13-year-old daughter had a "bad attitude." The parents had difficulty pinpointing specific behaviors that constituted a "good" or "bad" attitude, but both agreed that overall it had to do with their daughter's tone of voice, posture, and positive or negative verbalizations. Initially, the therapist asked the parents to use this global rating of the "quality" of the girl's interactions, recorded on a 3-point scale. The father, who was the primary caregiver, recorded an overall rating for each day, while the mother recorded only on days when she had more time with the adolescent. When the family returned to clinic, it was noted that the father and mother did not usually agree on the girl's attitude, allowing the therapist to help them come up with a clearer definition of "attitude" and to probe into possible discrepancies in the parents' expectations. This was followed by more precise recording of specific "attitude" behaviors.

A Special Kind of Quality Recording: Task Achievement

Sometimes therapists may be interested in documenting a person's progress in learning a set of new skills. Rather than measure how often, how quickly, how long, or how well the person emits the target behavior, perhaps they just want to document that he or she has finally emitted it, that he or she has passed certain milestones of achievement. By showing that passage and the date on which it occurred, they may be able to depict his or her progress adequately for their purposes.

For example, suppose that a teacher is instructing a child to discriminate (in this case, name) the colors in a set of six crayons. Of course the teacher knows that he or she has not mastered, say, "red" just because the child said "red" once when the red crayon was held up; the teacher will use a higher criterion than that. The teacher might decide that the child has met the criterion for "knowing" the color red when he or she correctly names the red crayon on 10 successive presentations, with no corrections or hints from the teacher and with other colors interspersed between presentations of red.

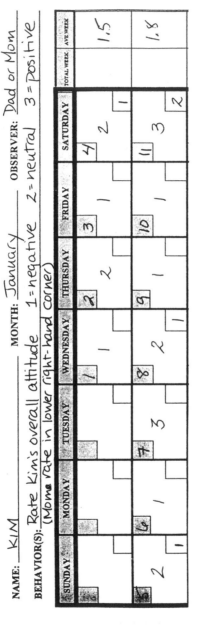

Figure 14. Quality recording: a 13-year-old girl's "attitude," rated overall for the day by her parents. (Form 12 in Appendix.) *Comments:* The father, who was the primary caregiver, rated the girl's "attitude" on a 3-point scale (1 = negative; 2 = neutral; 3 = positive) daily. The mother served as a reliability check by recording in the lower right-hand corner her ratings on the weekends and whenever she had opportunity to observe. In this form, the clinician adapted a monthly calendar, writing the date in the shaded upper left-hand corner of each day. As a means of giving immediate feedback to the family during clinic sessions, the therapist averaged the father's ratings for the week and asked for further information on the bases for the ratings.

The teacher might not be concerned about the child later forgetting, but if he or she is concerned, the criterion could be changed to correctly naming the color on 10 trials in each of 2 sessions, with no corrections and with no errors. Additionally, a time criterion can be set, such as within 2 seconds. The criteria depend on how fluent the teacher thinks the child needs to be at that task at this point in his or her life.

One can simply record, for each training session, whether the child met the criteria for correct naming of any color during that session, and if she did, what the colors were. Once she has met the criteria for a particular color, it is not necessary to record anything about her naming of that color in subsequent sessions; the naming of that color is considered to be mastered.

In another example, a 9-year-old girl seen in clinic had a dental phobia. When she sat in the dental chair, she would immediately begin to gag. Being touched on the face by the dentist elicited vomiting. To treat this problem, a hierarchy of progressively more aversive stimuli was developed with the girl. She was then taught progressive muscle relaxation and treatment entailed graduated exposure to the stimuli along the hierarchy while she remained relaxed. Criteria were set for "mastery" of each step in the hierarchy.

Her achievement of these steps was recorded by simply indicating, for each of the situations listed on the checklist in Figure 15, on what date she achieved a step and the SUDS rating she gave it at the end of 30 seconds of exposure. The SUDS rating was obtained at the first exposure to the step and when the step was achieved.

From these raw data, a graph of progress was then drawn. As the girl achieved the criterion to a situation—3 consecutive sessions with no gagging/vomiting and a SUDS rating at or below 3 on a 10-point scale—an X was placed beside that situation and above the week in which the criterion was met. This is illustrated in Figure 16.

This is a type of quality recording because the behavior must meet certain "quality" criteria (absence of gagging/vomiting and SUDS rating) to be considered achieved. Notice the resemblance of this to noting whether a child has cleaned his or her room by checking off the presence or absence of a set of components that, together, constitute a clean room. The difference between task-achievement recording and most quality-recording checklists is that, with the former, one is interested only in when the person passes from nonmastery of the component subtasks to mastery, whereas, with most quality-recording checklists, *daily* performance of a set of skills that the person already mastered is measured.

Cue-Effectiveness Recording

This recording method often overlaps with other methods, but it is included here to be sure that certain valuable possibilities are not overlooked. Sometimes

NAME: _Claire_

HIERARCHY OF VISIT TO DENTIST

SITUATION:	DATE DONE	SUDS 1-10 (1ˢᵗ time)	SUDS 1-10 (last time)
CLINIC: 1. Enter clinic	3 -16	9	2
2. Enter dental suite	3 -30	10	1
3. Sit in dental chair	4 - 6	9	3
DENTIST, NO INSTRUMENT 4. Dentist enters room	4 -13	8	2
5. Touches face (no gloves)	4 -27	10	3
6. Touches face (gloves)	5 -11	9	2
7. Touches lip			
8. Touches front tooth			
9. Touches teeth on outside			
10. Touches tongue			
11. Touches teeth on inside			
12. Touches tongue & teeth randomly			
MIRROR 13. Touches face			
14. Touches mouth			
15. Touches tongue			
16. Touches tongue & teeth randomly			
PROBE 17. Touches tongue & teeth randomly			
DRILL OFF 18. Touches tongue & teeth randomly			
DRILL ON (NO BIT) 19. Touches tongue & teeth randomly			

Figure 15. Task achievement checklist of steps in repeated exposure hierarchy for a 9-year-old girl with a dental phobia. (Adaptation of Form 1 in Appendix.) *Comments:* The clinician recorded the date a step was achieved, the SUDS rating of anxiety (1–10) on the first exposure of each step, and when the step was achieved (last time). These were then graphed, as can be seen in Figure 16.

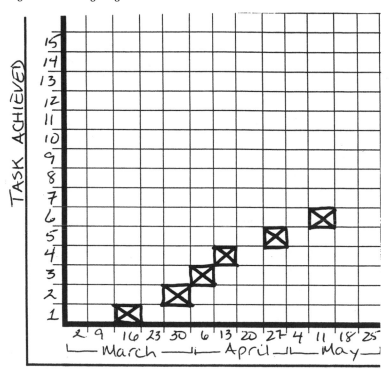

Figure 16. Graph of tasks achieved in repeated exposure hierarchy for a 9-year-old girl with a dental phobia. (Form 6 in Appendix.) *Comments:* See Figure 15 for the steps in the hierarchy. Steps are listed along the Y-axis, with dates achieved along the X-axis. Each time a step was achieved, the therapist filled in the block corresponding to the date when achieved. If a step was not achieved in a session, the square was left blank on the form.

what you are interested in developing is not more frequent occurrence of the target behavior (frequency or interval recording), longer occurrence of the target behavior (duration recording or momentary time sampling), quicker occurrence of the behavior (latency recording), or more accurate performance (quality recording), but more consistent occurrence of the behavior *when the cues occur that should evoke that behavior.* "Opportunities to respond," as described previously in this book are such "cues." For example, if the therapist were interested in a shy child's answering a teacher's questions in school, he or she needs to know how often the child offers to answer, *given that the teacher has asked a question.* The teacher's question is the cue, the stimulus that hopefully will be discriminative for the child's hand-raising behavior. Someone might write a number each time the teacher asks a question—"1" for the first, "2" for the second, etc.—and then circle the number if the target child does raise his or her hand to answer. This recording could be done by the teacher, but it is hard to carry on a discussion and do that re-cording at the same time, so a peer or older child would probably be the best choice, and the recording could also be done only every third day or so, to make the data-collection burden light and yet get frequent enough information to serve the clinical purposes.

Another example might be to measure how regularly a child obeys a parent's commands and requests. The parent could record each occurrence of a command/request the same way that the teacher's questions were recorded. Then he or she could circle the number if the child began complying within a certain time—such as 10 seconds—and cross it out if the child did not. Notice that the parent must not repeat the command until the time for compliance has passed. When such a repeat command is given, the prior command is recorded as disobeyed (or at least ig-nored) and the repeat is counted as a further command. Of course, in some cases the clinician may want to know just what the commands were without burdening the parent with too much data collection. A solution is to have the parent write ver-batim the first three (or whatever number) commands of the day.

Figure 17 gives an example of a clinic-based measure of compliance. Sev-eral methods have been developed, such as filling in three lines of blocked squares in 1-minute intervals (Forehand & McMahon, 1981). This method is somewhat time-consuming and takes practice to become fluent in, but it gives a clear picture of child compliance/noncompliance. The clinician calculates the percent of com-mands complied with ("percent compliance"), which can then be graphed after each session. Figure 18 uses the format of Barkley (1987), where the first five com-mands in every minute are recorded. The code gives less information than the Forehand and McMahon code, but is easier for a clinician to use without training. As with Figure 17, the clinician calculates the percent compliance and graphs that over the course of treatment.

Figure 19 gives another example of cue-effectiveness recording used in clinic. In this example, the child is learning to spoonfeed. The steps in the task are listed at the top. With each instruction, the response is indicated as incorrect, prompted, approximate, or correct. The number of trials is listed and then percent correct calculated. Note that the task is taught in a backward chaining fashion (i.e., step 6 is taught first). This type of record is useful when a teacher has set a learning criterion and wants to be sure the child has learned one step before moving to the next. This kind of precision is very helpful when setting individualized education plan goals, where it is hoped that the teacher will change goals and adapt teaching if criteria are not being met.

Conclusion

Whatever the method of recording, remember that it can be changed if the method turns out not to serve one's current purposes well. Most of the time, the primary

C. High Demand Parent-Child Interaction: "Ask your child to do several things, about four or five every minute. Begin by asking him/her to pick up the toys."

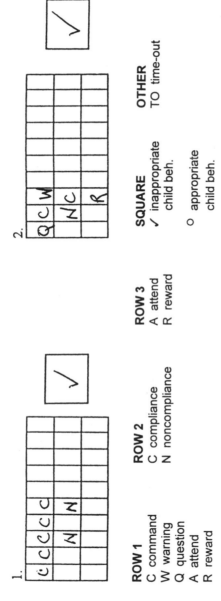

ROW 1	ROW 2	ROW 3
C command	C compliance	A attend
W warning	N noncompliance	R reward
Q question		
A attend		
R reward		

SQUARE	OTHER
✓ inappropriate child beh.	TO time-out
O appropriate child beh.	

Figure 17. Cue-effectiveness recording: Compliance in response to commands given. (Reprinted with permission from Guilford Press from McMahon & Forehand, 1981.) *Comments:* Each block of squares represents one minute. The first row codes parent commands; the second row codes child compliance/noncompliance, and the third row indicates parent responses. Any child negative behavior any time during the minute interval is indicated by a check in the separate square to the right. Percent compliance is then calculated as (child complies/complies plus noncomplies) × 100. In this example, the compliance rate is 25%. This form can be adapted to other behavior, such as aggression. This is the same parent–child interaction as shown in Figure18. A detailed explanation of the original code using this format may be found in the Forehand & McMahon (1981) text.

C. High Demand Parent-Child Interaction: "Ask your child to do several things, about four or five every minute. Begin by asking him/her to pick up the toys."

CODING FORM FOR RECORDING PARENT-CHILD INTERACTIONS

min.	1 Par.	1 Child	1 Par.	2 Par.	2 Child	2 Par.	3 Par.	3 Child	3 Par.	4 Par.	4 Child	4 Par.	5 Par.	5 Child	5 Par.
1	C R R R R R R R R	Cpy Ncpy Neg	A PNeg	C R R R R R R R R	Cpy Ncpy Neg	A PNeg	C R R R R R R R R	Cpy Ncpy Neg	A PNeg	C R R R R R R R R	Cpy Ncpy Neg	A PNeg	C R R R R R R R R	Cpy Ncpy Neg	A PNeg
2	C R R R R R R R R	Cpy Ncpy Neg	A PNeg	C R R R R R R R R	Cpy Ncpy Neg	A PNeg	C R R R R R R R R	Cpy Ncpy Neg	A PNeg	C R R R R R R R R	Cpy Ncpy Neg	A PNeg	C R R R R R R R R	Cpy Ncpy Neg	A PNeg

Abbreviations: Par. = parent; C = parent original command; R = parent repeat command; Cpy = compiliance within 10 seconds; Ncpy = noncompliance (failure to comply in 10 seconds); Neg = child negative behavior; A = parent approval and praise; PNeg = parent negative behavior.

Figure 18. Cue-effectiveness recording: Compliance in response to commands given. (Reprinted with permission from Guilford Press from Barkley, 1987.) *Comments:* This is the form used by Russell Barkley (1987), where the first five commands in every minute are recorded. This is the same parent–child interaction as shown in Figure 17. The overall compliance rate is 25%. The reader is referred to Barkley's text for a more complete form and operational definitions.

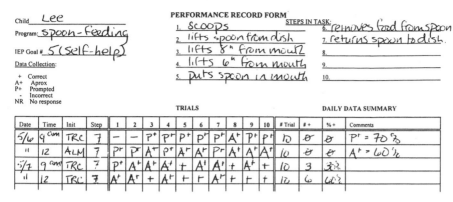

Figure 19. Performance record: Spoonfeeding. (Form 30 in Appendix.) *Comments:* The steps in the task are listed at the top. With each cue to take a bite, the response is indicated as incorrect (−), prompted (P+), approximate (A+), or correct (+). The number of trials was listed and then percent correct calculated. Prompted or approximate responses were calculated separately under comments. In this particular example, the criterion for moving on to the next step was 9 out of 10 trials correct without prompting.

purpose will be to get quantitative clinical information that is accurate and frequent enough to keep the clinician and the family adequately apprized of the current status of the case and the rate of change. If the data indicate that the case is progressing well, the data will reinforce the clinician's and family's persistence. If the data say that progress is negative or too slow, they are a cue to make adjustments in the treatments being used. Sometimes the primary purpose may be to see if the youth or family will follow through on any procedure, in order to determine the likelihood that treatment procedures will get implemented. Other times, the primary purpose of data collection may be to cue the child, parents, or teachers to implement certain procedures consistently or merely to get focused on specific goals. In all cases, defining target behaviors, collecting quantitative clinical information, graphing the data, and perusing the graphs with clients are likely to provide the most beneficial treatment outcomes.

Using Checklists and Rating Scales

This chapter is about two further ways to measure behavior (and other events): checklists and rating scales. These two methods are less precise and accurate than the direct, immediate measurements described in Chapter 3, yet usually less labor-intensive and often sufficiently precise and accurate for certain clinical purposes. In practice, checklists and rating scales blend into one another, but for the sake of clarity, they will be discussed separately here.

CHECKLISTS

A checklist is a list of events or characteristics on which a observer can indicate, by a check mark, whether the event or characteristic of interest did occur or is present. There are many kinds of checklists with various purposes. Many checklists are useful for initial assessment—for deciding on the nature of the problem and selecting target behaviors, persons, or other variables—or for pre–post measurement. However, only checklists with certain characteristics would be promising for monitoring progress (cf. Hawkins, 1979), as recommended in this book. Five important characteristics will be described, the first two of which overlap one another.

Objective Description

The behaviors (or situations) listed on the checklist should be specified in objective terms, not inferential ones. For example, suppose the checklist says "paying attention to teacher." How does a teacher know when the student is "paying attention"? Obviously, the teacher must infer that from what the student does, from the student's behavior. But, if those student behaviors are not specified on the checklist, there is no objective measure, instead the teacher's subjective judgment is being measured and the clinician will not know what student behaviors that

judgment is based upon. The teacher may judge that the student was "paying attention" because the student looked when he or she was giving an instruction. Or, the
teacher may not consider the student to be paying attention unless the student nods
or says he or she understands. On the other hand, the criterion may be that the student follows the teacher's instruction accurately.

Most likely the most desirable information is whether the student followed
the instruction, or perhaps partially followed it, but whatever you want to know is
what the checklist should ask. Otherwise, it may not be an accurate and sensitive
measure of the child's progress.

To illustrate, it is far more objective to list the behavior "apologized when
appropriate (e.g., when hurt someone's feelings, did something rude)" than to list
"felt sorry when he hurt someone's feelings or was rude." This latter is an infer-
ence, because what someone is feeling cannot reliably be determined. To illustrate
further, suppose the clinician is addressing how well a previously abusive parent is
now dealing with his or her child's misbehavior. The clinician has decided that it is
important for the parent to react to the misbehavior immediately, rather than wait
until it recurs and he or she is angry and risks overreacting. Perhaps a checklist is to
be completed every time the child misbehaves, so the clinician has a record of the
parent's reaction to each occasion of misbehavior. One item on the checklist might
be "responded to the misbehavior the first time it occurred and within 5 seconds."
Then there would be a "yes" column and a "no" column beside this, as well as other
component behaviors, and the data collector (perhaps the parent, the clinician, or a
reliable relative) would check the appropriate column. Thus, the behavioral objectives have been defined clearly and can be measured objectively.

Precise, Specific; Not Global

In the preceding example, notice how much better it is to record specific responses, as a measure of progress, than to try measuring a global summary or an
impressionistic characteristic like "deals with misbehavior in a timely manner."
While the global, impressionistic measurement may be efficient for initial,
preintervention assessment of the nature of the problem, it is poor for monitoring
progress. Most behaviors in a checklist used for monitoring progress should be described in specific terms, not as fuzzy concepts.

For example, an item like "is dependent" is not only subjective—meaning
different behaviors to different people—but also global, because it can mean numerous different behaviors in numerous different situations. It would be much
better if the checklist included several specific behaviors that were meant by the
concept, such as "stayed too close to mother for a child his age," or the opposite,
"participated readily in play with peers." These dependent behaviors can be listed
under a heading, such as "dependent versus independent," but the heading itself is
too inclusive and vague to be reliably checked as "present" versus "absent."

Worded as an Event, Not a Characteristic

Ideally, a progress-monitoring checklist item refers to a specific event, not a characteristic of many repetitions of that event. For example, although it is appropriate to know whether a school child is "attentive to teacher," "speaks loud enough," or "is friendly," those wordings do not refer to one specific occurrence. They are not discrete events, but rather enduring qualities of behaviors. They are best suited to rating scales, especially ones that are to be used only occasionally, such as monthly or pre–post treatment.

Since such infrequent measurement is not useful for monitoring progress, it would be best to find a way to convert the item into specific behaviors that can be included in a checklist or into one of the measurement methods discussed in Chapter 3. Suppose, for example, the therapist was interested in how well an 8-year-old named Ted cooperated with his older sister when she was in charge after school each day. Of course, the parents could be asked to provide a global daily rating of Ted's being "cooperative with his older sister," but it would be better to list the specific behaviors that the parents wish to change (and probably relevant situations). These, then, can be made into a checklist to be completed daily by the data collector(s).

To illustrate, one item that might be included is "follows sister's reasonable requests/commands." Each evening, the parents would review Ted's behavior with his sister and decide whether she was correct in checking "yes" or "no" for that behavior on the checklist. There would, no doubt, be several other "cooperative" behaviors on the checklist, perhaps including a global or "miscellaneous" one, and a decision would be made each evening regarding how to check each behavior listed.

Individualized (Ideographic) Items

A progress-monitoring device is going to be most relevant for a specific case and most sensitive as an indicator of progress if it is developed for that specific case. Thus, a clinician should not despair if there is no standardized measurement device already available. This book is not about standardized, general assessment devices. Even a device developed for a specific *type* of problem is still not as sensitive and complete as one that a clinician develops for the individual case, although it is considerably better than a device developed for assessing a wide range of problems. A clinician might choose to use parts of a prepared checklist that seems especially relevant and, based on those, develop an individualized checklist (or rating scale). And, it may still be supplemented with further items that will reflect the behaviors and situations of interest with the individual client.

Figure 20 gives an example of a very simple checklist used as a school-home note (cf. Kelley, 1990). The teacher checks off each behavior at the end of a speci-

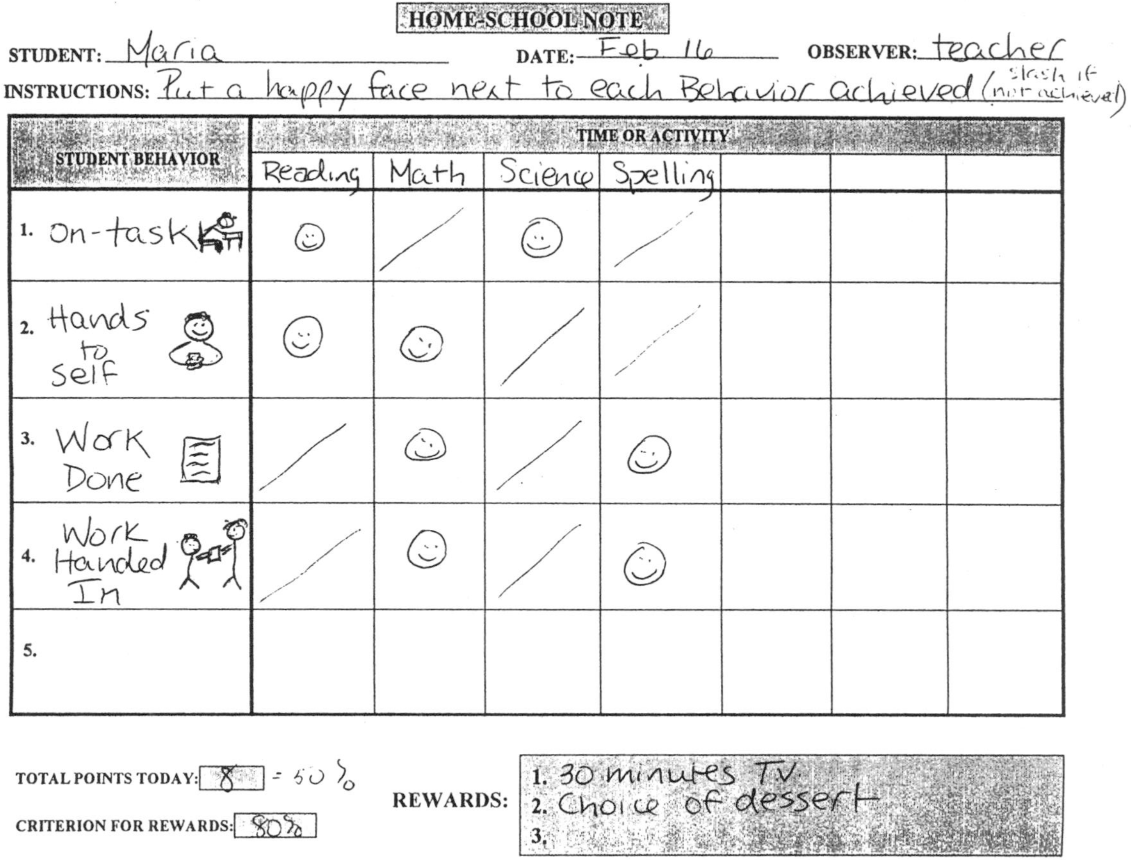

HOME-SCHOOL NOTE

STUDENT: Maria DATE: Feb 16 OBSERVER: teacher

INSTRUCTIONS: Put a happy face next to each Behavior achieved (slash if not achieved)

STUDENT BEHAVIOR	TIME OR ACTIVITY						
	Reading	Math	Science	Spelling			
1. On-task	☺	/	☺	/			
2. Hands to Self	☺	☺	/	/			
3. Work Done	/	☺	/	☺			
4. Work Handed In	/	☺	/	☺			
5.							

TOTAL POINTS TODAY: 8 = 50%

CRITERION FOR REWARDS: 80%

REWARDS:
1. 30 minutes TV
2. Choice of dessert
3.

Figure 20. Checklist of school behavior across activities (using a pictogram). (Form 23 in Appendix.) *Comments:* Maria's teacher gave happy faces when the behavior was observed during the specific academic period. If she did *not* show in the targeted behavior, a slash was drawn through the square. When Maria got home, her parents counted the total points, calculated the percent of points earned (# of happy faces/ # of happy faces + # of slashes × 100) and delivered rewards if appropriate.

fied activity and sends the recording sheet home at the end of the day. The parents then deliver a reward at home for meeting a specific criterion (usually 70–80%, at least initially). In this particular case, the teacher recorded whether each of four target behaviors occurred during four academic periods. Pictograms were used as names for the behaviors because of Maria's reading difficulties. Happy faces were used for occurrence of the behaviors, and a slash was used when they were not achieved. Maria brought the form home, the parents reviewed the percentage of points with her, and delivered one of the rewards listed if she met the criterion shown on the note. Sometimes Maria failed to bring home the sheet and reported to the parents that the sheet was lost, so the parents delivered a reward based on her verbal report of meeting criterion. In was discovered, however, that these were times when she did *not* meet criterion and was trying to manipulate the system. Consequently, the rule was set that the parents would *only* deliver rewards if the form was returned to them and initialed by the teacher.

Brief, Simple Items

Obviously, if a checklist is too long or complex, it will not be completed consistently and thoughtfully by the observer. Thus, it is best to make individualized checklists as brief and relevant as possible.

RATING SCALES

Usually the term "rating scale" implies that a continuous dimension is being measured by the scale. "Loud enough," "politely," "angrily," "enthusiastic," and "impulsive" could all be considered continuous dimensions of behavior and could appear on a rating scale. For example, a rating scale might ask "How interested did he or she appear in _____?" or "How frightened did he or she act regarding ____ _____?" The observer would then provide a rating indicating how much the term "interested" or "frightened" seemed applicable to the behavior that he or she observed.

Notice that the data collector's rating is presumably based on specific behaviors that he or she has observed, often several behaviors. For example, a rating of "How anxious did you feel?" involves the respondent's integrating his or her observations of his or her own heart rate, stomach tightening, trembling, perspiring, avoiding of a stimulus, and so on. Obviously, this is a subjective measurement. If, in addition, the person is asked to integrate these observations across several occasions, the subjectivity of rating is increased. This creates great opportunity for irrelevant factors to influence the data, factors such as the data collector's wanting to please the clinician, place him or herself in a favorable light, or make someone look better or worse than they really are. Therefore, we are generally less enthusiastic about rating scales for monitoring progress than we are about checklists, but they do have an important place.

In most clinical practice, there are some events and conditions that can best be measured by a rating scale. Both anxiety and pain are good examples. Other more objective measures can supplement a rating, such as physiological measures and the number of activities missed due to pain or anxiety. If a significant part of a child's problem is related to pain, it might be appropriate to have him or her rate the pain at certain times throughout the day. Because even the most conscientious person has difficulty recalling distant information, it is not likely to be beneficial to ask for a global rating such as "How often did you experience pain this week" or even "How bad was the pain you experienced today?" Requiring the data collector to recall past events—especially ones that are days old or that are easy to forget—invites inaccuracy and bias.

Figure 21 gives an example of a pain rating scale (Allen & Mathews, 1998) used in a case of an adolescent girl who was asked to rate her pain at four predetermined times daily. The ratings are then connected to make a graph of pain ratings over the course of the day. Some youths like to connect the points with a curve rather than a straight line so that they can indicate fluctuations between points. Note Rachelle also indicated missed activities and medications taken, which are not only more objective but also indicate the severity in *functional* terms.

WHEN TO MEASURE

How often to measure when using a checklist or rating scale depends on how the items are worded and how quickly the problem is likely to abate. If it is expected that there will be improvement within a month or less, daily measurement is probably best. If it is likely to take 6 months or more, measurement one day per week might give quick enough feedback and sensitive enough monitoring. Whatever the frequency, the items should refer to "now," not to numerous occasions, even such as "today" or certainly not to "over the past week."

Specific times to measure depend both on when the opportunities for the behavior are maximal and such practical matters as when the data collector is available and whether he or she must travel to get to the child. As with the methods described in Chapter 3, it may not make sense to measure the behavior at all times. Cooperation and more careful measurement will generally be better if the observer is only asked to assess at certain moments or for certain portions of the time. For example, a rating of how a child is engaged with his or her schoolwork at *several predetermined moments or activities* each day (not known to the child in advance, of course) should provide an adequate sample. Similarly, a checklist of how many polite behaviors a child showed *at mealtime* and at *one other selected time or activity* might give a good sample of whether the child is progressing.

WEEKLY PAIN RECORD

Name __Rachelle_____ Age _11o_ Sex: Male (Female)

INTENSITY - Four times each day, please update the pain graph according to the following scale.

I N T E N S I T Y

(0) NO PAIN
(1)
(2) SLIGHTLY PAINFUL - I only notice my pain when I focus my attention on it.
(3)
(4) MILDLY PAINFUL - I can ignore my pain most of the time.
(5)
(6) PAINFUL - It is painful, but I can continue what I am doing.
(7)
(8) VERY PAINFUL - My pain makes concentration difficult, but I can perform undemanding tasks.
(9)
(10) EXTREMELY PAINFUL - I can't do anything when I have such pain.

MEDICATION - Each time you take medication for pain, please indicate the type and amount of medication.

MONDAY (Date 5-15)

MEDICATION (type and amount)

None

School Missed? Yes (No)
Classes Missed:
none

Activities Missed: none

TUESDAY (Date 5-16)

MEDICATION (type and amount)

School Missed? Yes (No)
Classes Missed:
none

Activities Missed: none

WEDNESDAY (Date 5-17)

MEDICATION (type and amount)

Ibuprofen, 400 mg

School Missed? (Yes) No ½ day
Classes Missed:
Math, Science, Lunch,
Study Hall
Activities Missed: Soccer

OVER

Figure 21. Pain intensity ratings. (Form 26 in Appendix.) *Comments:* Rachelle rated her headaches at four set times during the day, then completed information on medication and school or social acitivities missed. She chose to connect the points in a linear fashion, but was given the option of using a curved line to indicate fluctuations between recordings.

CONCLUSION

There are many existing checklists and rating scales, and many of them are very useful for *initial assessment*, when roughly trying to determine the problems and their severity. But, for monitoring progress, a device needs to be objective, narrowly focused, behaviorally precise, individually tailored, and brief. It is usually best to individualize a scale, as it is usually most sensitive to the changes the therapist is attempting to achieve in this particular case. Normative standardization is not important for such use, partly because it inevitably detracts from individualization, and thus, sensitivity.

The checklist for monitoring progress will usually be shorter than the one used for initial assessment, and thus more likely to be completed by the observer at the desired time. Adopting or adapting items from existing checklists or rating scales can be an efficient way to construct a device for monitoring progress, but be sure that the items contain everything needed.

The measurement should be done at frequencies that can quickly represent the overall change in the behaviors measured, but practical considerations may force the clinician to compromise somewhat on the frequency and comprehensiveness of the samples. If the clinician is unsure whether the information does represent overall progress, a simple form can be added on which the child or parent rates, daily or weekly, how representative the quantitative information is of the child's overall behavior or his or her behavior at other times and places.

Arranging the Data in Graphs

To maximize the benefits of data, they need to be arranged in a way that the "consumer"—e.g., the clinician, family members, teacher, clinical supervisor, case manager for a managed care agency—can make best use of them. Usually, the best arrangement of quantitative information is to graph it.

Graphs have several advantages. First, *a graph consolidates the data into a compact form* that constitutes an *instantly interpreted* picture of the child's status and progress. Consider how much less time it takes to "read" a simple, clear graph than to read the numbers it represents. The "height" of the data on some problem behavior indicates how serious the problem is at any point in time; the direction of slope (trend) in the data across time indicates whether the child is progressing, regressing, or staying constant; and the steepness of the slope indicates how fast he or she is progressing. The whole process of collecting and graphing data can be conceptualized as "drawing a picture of the client's problem, across time." No client retrospective impressions, tests, or clinician's ratings can provide as precise and credible evidence. Sometimes a child or parent will even say that things are going well or that they are going poorly, yet the data will contradict that conclusion.

Second, *inspecting the graph with the child and parents keeps everyone focused on specific goals* and thus avoids getting distracted by myriad other issues and current complaints. Most children and parents have many things they would like to tell a clinician, and it is easy to get sidetracked by the constantly changing issues in their lives.

Third, *the highs and lows in performance will be immediately apparent on the graph* and can cue the clinician to inquire about events on those particular days. This can lead to a better understanding of the environmental and biological factors that influence the target behavior.

Fourth, *the graph provides feedback to the parents* that can serve to reinforce their hard work or cue them to buckle down. Of course, the graph can be an important reinforcer for the clinician as well.

Fifth, *a graph can be used to persuade others that they should join in the efforts* that the clinician and the family have been engaged in. For example, the graph may convince a spouse, grandparent, teacher, or sibling that therapy is worthwhile and deserves their involvement.

Finally, of course, *a graph can be used to quickly show a managed care company, a supervisor, or other such outside party* that the clinician is doing good work. While tables of data or even stacks of data sheets can serve some of these purposes, only graphs can serve all of them with maximal effectiveness and efficiency.

CHARACTERISTICS OF A GRAPH

As mentioned previously, graphs are pictorial in nature. They usually involve two reference lines that intersect at a 90 degree angle. The lower, horizontal line (the abscissa) usually describes the time unit, such as days, weeks, or training sessions. The left-hand, vertical line (the ordinate) describes the measurement units by which the target behavior is being evaluated, such as the frequency of hits, the number of hours of TV viewing, or the percent of intervals showing the target behavior.

It is a good idea to keep pencil-drawn, "working" graphs of each behavior being recorded. Don't worry about making them glamorous; if that becomes important at some point, they can be regraphed more formally at that time (provided the numbers themselves have been kept). In fact, we recommend writing notes right on those working graphs indicating where certain potentially important events happen, such as the family's moving, a change in the treatment, a car accident, someone's being sick, etc. These notes can prove useful in analyzing what is influencing either the target behavior or something else that, in turn, influences the target behavior. The notes should not dominate, however; the data are what should stand out.

METHODS OF GRAPHING

The three most common types of graph are polygon, cumulative, and bar. The polygon is the one used most often. The choice of graphing method will probably be obvious and may require little thought. Factors that might influence the choice include the type of measurement used, the frequency of the behaviors or other events being graphed, the rapidity with which change occurs, the precision desired in examining the data, the clarity of the pictorial representation wanted, and the clinician's personal preference.

Polygon graphs (also called *frequency polygons*) are the very familiar ones in which data are plotted as specific points and the points are then connected by lines, like a dot-to-dot drawing, as shown in Figures 22 and 23. (See also the case studies presented in Chapter 9.)

Figure 22 presents the numerical data on a child's wetting her pants. The father simply put a tally mark for each time she wet her pants during the day. In some instances, the clinician may want more precision by getting the times of day that the father found wet pants, but the therapist decided that Genie's father would be more likely to keep the data if simplified. Figure 23 shows how these same data can be graphed as a polygon. Each data point represents the behavior during a particular unit of time, usually a day or a week. When the data points are connected by a line, the line's slope shows both the direction of change and the speed of change. Notice that the graph makes it immediately obvious whether the child is progressing and how rapidly, whereas raw data forms must be examined more carefully to detect that information.

Also notice that when data were not available for certain weeks, as often happens in clinical practice, two slashes were drawn through the data line so that it is obvious, pictorially, that there was an interruption of data collecting at that time. Finally, notice that the father collected baseline data in this case—something that is not always possible or desirable in clinical service delivery—and that the data point from baseline was not connected to those from the treatment condition, to emphasize the environmental changes made when treatment began.

Finally, notice that the clinician has written notes on the graph about events that could influence the behavior. This includes changes in the treatment procedures, of course. It is important to remember that this is not intended as a scientific experiment, in which the treatment might have to be kept constant even though that did not appear to be the best service to the client. The purpose of these data is to *enhance* clinical services and one's accountability, not to prove what caused what.

━━━━━━━━━━━━━━━━━━━━ Cumulative Graph

The datum plotted on a cumulative graph—also called a cumulative record—each day (or other relevant time unit) tells the *total* number of times the behavior has occurred *to date*. That is, the data keep accumulating, adding up from one time unit to the next. Figure 24 shows the same data depicted in Figure 23, but plotted cumulatively, with the total number of wets to date being plotted each week. They could also have been plotted day by day. This is sometimes useful for very infrequent behaviors, such as fire-setting or theft. While one can also plot cumulative duration or even latency, it would be rare for this to be useful.

NAME: Genie MONTH: Feb. OBSERVER: Dad

BEHAVIOR(S): # wets during daytime

<table>
<tr><th>SUNDAY</th><th>MONDAY</th><th>TUESDAY</th><th>WEDNESDAY</th><th>THURSDAY</th><th>FRIDAY</th><th>SATURDAY</th></tr>
<tr><td>1
|||
3</td><td>2
||
2</td><td>3
|
1</td><td>4
||
2</td><td>5
|||
3</td><td>6
|||
3</td><td>7
||
2</td></tr>
<tr><td>8
||
2</td><td>9
|
1</td><td>10
||
2</td><td>11
||
2</td><td>12
|
1</td><td>13
||
2</td><td>14
|
1</td></tr>
<tr><td>15
|
1</td><td>16
||
2</td><td>17
|
1</td><td>18
|
1</td><td>19
0
0</td><td>20
|
1</td><td>21
0
0</td></tr>
<tr><td>22
|
1</td><td>23
0
0</td><td>24
0
0</td><td>25
|
1</td><td>26
0
0</td><td>27
|
1</td><td>28
0
0</td></tr>
</table>

Figure 22. Raw data on the frequency of diurnal enuresis for Genie. (Form 12 in Appendix.) *Comments:* Genie's father recorded with tally marks on the calendar each time she wet her pants on a monthly calendar. The total number of wets was summarized in the lower right-hand corner of each day.

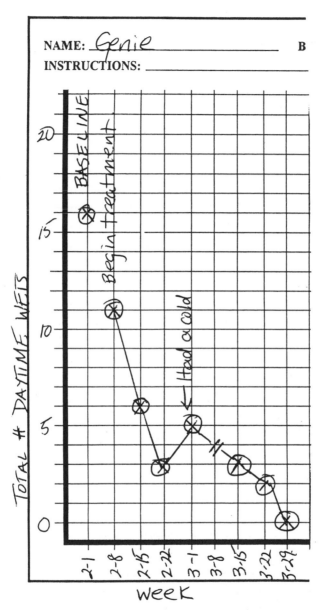

NAME: _Genie_____ **B**

INSTRUCTIONS: _____

Figure 23. Polygon graph of diurnal enuresis for Genie. (Form 6 in Appendix.) *Comments:* The therapist graphed the total number of wets for the week, obtained from Genie's father's data in Figure 22. Slash marks during week 3–8 indicate that the father neglected to record data adequately during those weeks.

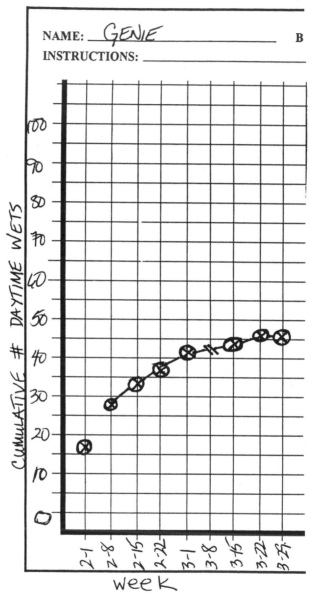

NAME: _GENIE_____ B

INSTRUCTIONS: _____

Figure 24. Cumulative graph of diurnal enuresis for Genie. (Form 6 in Appendix.) *Comments:* These are the same data seen in Figures 22 and 23. In this instance, however, the data continue to accumulate, each week's data are added on to the previous data. Note that Genie's progress seems less clear than in Figure 23. However, this type of graph can be very useful for task-achievement data (for example, see Figure 16).

A particularly promising use for cumulative graphs is when the child is acquiring a new set of skills in which each component skill is different from any other component, so that mastery of each component skill can be treated as a separate subskill. For example, suppose a child is initially acquiring expressive language, learning to spell a set of words, or learning a set of basic math problems. A cumulative graph can be used to show the child's improvement from having none of these component skills to having many. If there is a fixed number to be mastered, such as the basic multiplication facts ("times tables"), the graph will not only show the rate of the child's progress but also show when the child has mastered all of the component skills because the graph will reach its maximum.

Although cumulative graphs are excellent for plotting newly mastered subskills, they can have disadvantages for most purposes. Notice that the cumulative graph's data line cannot go down, since that would imply somehow subtracting a behavior that already occurred. Thus, the only slopes that the data line can take are those that fall within something less than a 90° angle. By contrast, a polygon's data line can go up or down and, thus, the slopes fall within something less than a 180° angle. One result is that any particular amount of behavior change deflects the cumulative graph's data line only half as much as it deflects the polygon's data line. This makes the cumulative graph give a less dramatic, less sensitive picture of changes in behavior across time compared to the polygon, although the careful reader will still see the change. A further result is that sometimes the graph must either be made very tall, made to use a very compressed vertical scale, or the data line must be "reset" to zero every time it reaches the top of the graph.

A second disadvantage of using the cumulative graph for purposes other than plotting newly mastered skills is that it can be hard for people to understand. Most people see polygons frequently in newspapers and magazines, but they see cumulative graphs less often. Thus, when the behavior that is being plotted fails to occur at all in a particular day (or other time unit) and the data line on the cumulative graph therefore stays at the same level or plateau, some readers will assume that this means the behavior stayed at the same level as on the previous day. In contrast, the polygon's data line would go down to zero and be easier to see as a reduced level of behavior.

Even when plotting the acquisition of new skills, a polygon is often better. For example, suppose a schoolchild is being taught a set of 90 basic multiplication facts. Suppose that on May 5 she gets all of them correct within the allotted time, but on May 6 she gets only 87 of them correct. There is no standard way to show that on a cumulative graph, since the behavior can only accumulate, not subtract.

Thus, if the primary interest is in how the learner performed from time unit to time unit, it is better to use a polygon; while if the primary interest is in showing the point at which she *first mastered* each of a set of skills, a cumulative graph can be best.

Of course, the criterion that defines "mastered" needs to be explicit. Sometimes "mastered" simply means "used correctly once." For example, if trying to develop a toddler's expressive language, a speech pathologist might write down each word he or she says each day (or on a predetermined day, or part of a day, each week). Every word he or she uses appropriately that is *new* can be added to the list of words he or she has already used correctly. The cumulative graph would then show the total number of words used correctly to date.

Bar Graph

In a bar graph, each datum is depicted by a single bar extending vertically from the abscissa. Such a graph might be useful if several behaviors are being compared during each time unit. In the earlier example of the child who wet her pants, the father was also asked to record the number of times the child urinated in the toilet. Figure 25 depicts both the desirable and the undesirable behaviors. Showing both behaviors makes the graph more revealing of what is happening.

However, it should be noted that the same data could have been plotted as a polygon. If this is desired, use a different type of data point for each behavior—perhaps a small open triangle for one and a closed circle for the other—and a different texture of data line, such as a dashed line for one and a solid line for the other.

As depicted in Figure 25, a bar graph can sometimes be produced automatically *while* recording the behavior, thus saving time and providing more immediate feedback to the child and family. Such automatic graphing is achieved by recording the data right on a sheet of squared (graph) paper. As a behavior occurs, an "X" is marked in a square directly above the time-unit marker on the abscissa or a square can be filled, perhaps by using a felt-tip marker. Subsequent occurrences are systematically marked one above the other, forming a vertical stack of X's or filled squares. This method is best used with frequency recording, although it could also be used with interval recording if the intervals are fairly large, such as an hour or more, so the data do not run off the top of the page quickly.

Graphs of Scores on Checklists or Rating Scales

Of course, data from checklists and rating scales can also be graphed. For example, a checklist of items that constitute a clean bedroom can be constructed, including items like "no foreign objects or materials on floor larger than an aspirin in size," "no more than seven items on dresser," and "each piece of furniture in its usual place." The clinician or a parent can graph either the number or the percent of items completed each day (perhaps by a certain time).

Data from a rating scale are likely to be easy to graph just as they are. If several ratings are made in a day, it is probably a good idea to graph the average rating each day. However, if one is interested in how the ratings change across the day (or

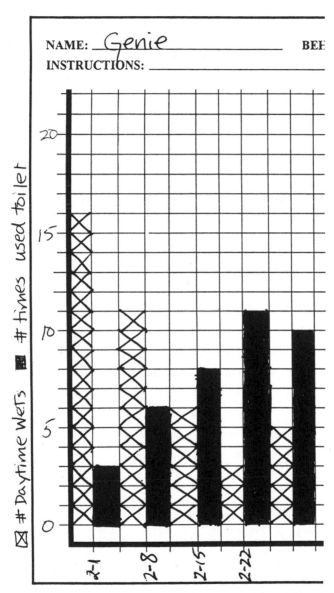

Figure 25. Genie: Bar graph of diurnal enuresis and frequency of urinating in toilet. (Form 6 in Appendix.) *Comments:* These are the same data plotted in Figures 23, 24, and 25. In this case, the father kept the data directly on the graph, by putting an "X" in each block cumulatively for the day. This also shows the number of times Genie used the toilet—the desirable alternative behavior.

other time period), it would also be advisable to construct a separate graph in which ratings from the same time of day on several days are averaged.

Indicating Criteria or Preset Goals on a Graph

Not only can a graph give the clinician and the family feedback on progress, it can help to clarify the parameters and goals of treatment. For instance, horizontal lines can be drawn to indicate sub-goals of treatment, just as an adolescent losing weight might draw a new horizontal line at the end of each month to indicate his or her weight goal for the next month. When the data line reaches the goal line for the month, indicating that the goal has been achieved, it can be quite reinforcing to everyone concerned: the child, the parents, the clinician, and any other professionals involved. However, it is also wise to add other reinforcers, such as special activities or permission to purchase a desired item.

Setting such intermediate goals is especially important when the behavior change is a difficult one to achieve. Of course, a line can also be drawn to show the *ultimate* goal of treatment—the outcome intended to be eventually achieved—but it is often unwise to do that before first achieving some intermediate goals, so that goals can be set realistically. Further, by continuing to track behavior after reaching the goal, one can see whether the behavior is being maintained at or above goal level.

It is usually helpful to set a "window of acceptable outcomes" when trying to reach and maintain a behavioral objective, that is a maximum and minimum that define the range that is acceptable. When the rate of improvement fails to point toward that window, the treatment program needs improvement. And when the objective is reached, continued data collection and graphing will show when the behavior gets outside of the window, suggesting the need to establish some kind of maintenance program.

Again, weight loss is a good example. Figure 26 is an example of a graph for weight loss in one adolescent girl. Her ultimate goal was to lose 40 pounds, but intermediate goals were set in 5-pound increments (indicated by a zigzag line) so that she would experience success and not get overwhelmed with the slow progress toward her final goal. The data are only partially depicted, for the sake of brevity, in this text. The full graph would show 10 months' worth of data, with changing criterion lines as she met 5-pound goals. After a 15-pound loss, she set the goal to maintain this weight for 4 weeks before setting a new 5-pound goal. Once she reached her ultimate goal of 125 pounds, a "window" was drawn, to allow her a range that she and the clinician considered acceptable for maintaining a healthy weight. For some adolescents, the reinforcement of weight loss can result in losing too much weight and setting unrealistic or unhealthy goals. Others may be in danger of gaining the weight back. Consequently, by setting an acceptable window, clients may relax the rigidity of the weight-loss program, but will then tighten up if they ap-

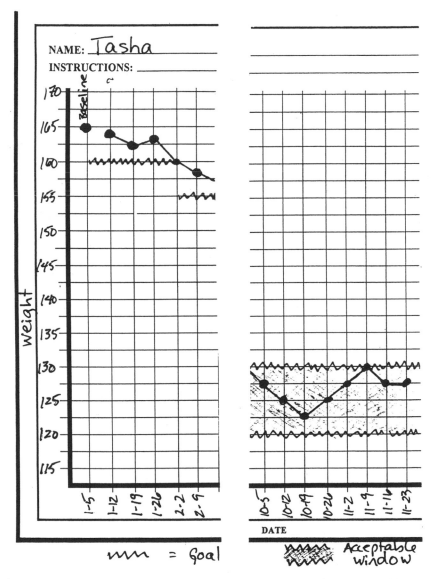

Figure 26. Graph of weight loss, with changing criteria and window of acceptable weight range. (Form 6 in Appendix.) *Comments:* This presents only two segments of a 10-month graph, with the beginning of treatment shown on the left and the end of treatment on the right. The zigzag line at the beginning of treatment indicates short-term goals, set in 5-pound increments. Once Tasha had met her long-term goal of 125 pounds, a "window" was set for weight maintenance. This is depicted by a shaded area, with zigzag lines as upper and lower limits of the window.

proach the limits shown by the window. Perhaps we should point out that weight is not actually a behavior: it is a *product* of such behaviors as choosing what foods to buy and eat, eating a certain amount, and exercising.

SUMMARY

Graphs provide instantly understandable pictures of behavior across time. Such pictures have several advantages over tables or other collections of data. It is usually important to keep a "working graph" of the data that is updated immediately when new data are available, so that the graph can affect the clinician's and client's behavior. Working graphs should be informal, not labor intensive, and it is appropriate and helpful to make notes about potentially important events on the graphs.

Frequency polygons are often the most useful graphs, but on occasion it may be beneficial to employ cumulative graphs, bar graphs, or types that are not described here. One type of bar graph is especially likely to be useful: that which is produced automatically during the recording of behavior by "building" X's or other marks that fill squares on graph paper.

It is desirable to draw short-term and, especially, long-term quantitative goals right on a graph, since these define what level one is attempting to reach. Though achievement of such goals themselves will serve as a reinforcer for everyone's hard work, other reinforcers should also be made available at such times. Of course, other, much more immediate (e.g., daily) reinforcers will also be crucial to the success of the treatment/teaching.

Engaging the Child and Family in Collecting and Using Clinical Data

Deciding to get quantitative clinical information will not necessarily ensure that successful data collection will occur, because the clinician usually must rely on others, such as the adolescent, parent, or teacher to gather the information. This chapter is oriented toward cases in which the child or someone in the child's daily life will be the data collector.

When children or others in their lives are to be the observers, the task of getting them to collect data is the same as the task of getting them to carry out their part of a treatment plan. The therapist must first convince them of the importance of getting and using quantitative information, then teach them how to get and use data, and finally motivate these behaviors throughout treatment. There are several aspects to this, and a clinician who ignores any of them will often find that the clients are not providing the necessary information.

Most clients do not come to us expecting to get data and know how valuable data will be, what would be worth monitoring, how those things might be measured in a credible way, or how to use the data after they are collected. Thus, although the clinician's task of getting them to record data can be simple, it can also be as difficult as getting clients to carry out a treatment "assignment."

ESTABLISH A THERAPEUTIC ALLIANCE WITH THE CHILD AND FAMILY

As mentioned in Chapter 2, in order to engage a child or parent in any part of the therapeutic process, one needs to first establish rapport and a therapeutic alliance—that is, to develop a therapist–client relationship in which everyone work as a team toward mutually agreed-upon goals. This process is far too complex to describe adequately here (see, e.g., Cormier & Cormier, 1979; DiGiuseppe et al.,

1996; Wright & Davis, 1994), but because of its relevance to collecting data, let us briefly mention a few factors.

Establish Rapport, So the Clinician Will Be Influential

First, building rapport involves interacting with the child and family in ways that encourage respect and trust (and—usually, but not necessarily—liking). This does not mean just being pleasant. It means such things as how intently the child's or parents' communication (verbal and nonverbal) is attended to; how "professional" the clinician's style is; how much empathic interest is shown in the family's feelings about things that have happened in their lives; how nonjudgmental the clinician is about their past behavior, feelings, possessions, etc.; how much awareness is shown of the person as a whole, while still keeping focused on the problem at hand; how reliably appointments are kept and tasks carried out by the clinician; how much the clinician emphasizes commonalities between him or herself and them; and the clinician's willingness to reveal minor aspects of his or her own life (without letting such revelations occupy much time). Even such trivial-seeming behavior as how the therapist stands, greets the child and family, uses humor, and recalls small things about the individual's life are important. Finally, inanimate factors can influence the client's trust and respect for the therapist, such as the appearance of his or her clothing and office.

These professional and personal behaviors lead the child, adolescent, or parent to be more truthful and nondefensive with the clinician and even with him or herself. They also lead to greater influence with the child and family. The client comes to care about whether the clinician approves or disapprove of something he or she says or does, and the clinician's genuine praise then becomes a reinforcer. Modeling, suggestions, directions, and even nonverbal cues also come to influence the child and family significantly; they become cues for attention and, often, compliance with agreed-upon assignments.

Reach a Therapeutic Alliance Regarding Quantitative Clinical Information

In conducting therapy, it is necessary to go one step further than establishing oneself as influential with clients—further than getting them to care "what you think." It is also necessary for them to be committed to *act*, to carry out tasks in their daily life that are unfamiliar and difficult. Unless they can do things differently in their daily life, the clinician really cannot help with their problems. This applies to data collection just as it does to carrying out therapeutic assignments.

To reach this therapeutic alliance regarding data collection, at least seven steps are recommended:

1	Be committed to and enthusiastic about getting and using quantitative clinical information.
2	Be prepared in advance.
3	Provide rationales that the child and family understand and appreciate.
4	Work out the precise nature of the tasks as a teammate with the clients.
5	Use simple procedures.
6	Teach them to carry out the tasks.
7	Get a commitment to carry out the tasks (on at least a trial basis).

Each step will be discussed here.

1. Be Committed to and Enthusiastic about Quantitative Clinical Information

A prerequisite for successful data collection is for the clinician to be convinced of the importance of such information and the use of this information throughout treatment. When the clinician is convinced, the child and family will detect it and more easily be convinced and motivated themselves. One way to demonstrate commitment is to begin collecting data in clinic during the first session, however crude or preliminary they are. For instance, while interviewing the parents, the clinician could keep a tally of the number of child interruptions or activity changes. If the parents are describing oppositional behavior, the clinician might ask the parents to give 10 commands and keep data on the complies and noncomplies. By then feeding back this information to the parents, the clinician has demonstrated that there is value in collecting quantitative information.

2. Be Prepared in Advance

It is important to be prepared for data collection before the family walks in the door for the first time (or the clinician walks in their door, if working in their natural environment). This would entail having a variety of devices and forms available—both generic and specific—that would be suitable for the types of families commonly seen. It would be advisable to keep an ongoing file or notebook of forms used in the past, because some of them will be useful again and again. If financially feasible, a computer program for creating forms would be a sound investment. New forms can be prepared before an appointment or, if necessary, while the family waits. It is useful to keep two or three generic forms on the clinician's clipboard, such as Form 1 (Generic Vertical Form), Form 4 (Generic Horizontal Form) and Form 6 (Graph) from the Appendix. These particular forms can easily be adapted on the spot.

Normally, it is advisable to *provide* recording forms and devices, rather than ask the client to create or procure them. Not only does providing forms communicate the clinician's seriousness about assigning this task, it improves the probability of the family's compliance because their effort has been reduced. On occasion, however, adolescents or their parents find it enjoyable to create their own forms, perhaps on a computer at home or at school. In this case, be sure to provide a clear model of what is needed.

Data collection devices that are expensive could be made available for sale or rent (probably with a damage deposit), while those that are less costly—such as a golf counter or pocket calendar—could be given to the family as part of clinical service. A good policy is to make use of devices that are the least costly while still ensuring the adequacy of data collection.

3. Provide Rationales that the Child and Family Can Understand, Appreciate, and Preferably Repeat

The child and family deserve a convincing explanation of the need for collecting data. Some of the rationale given in Chapter 1 should be useful; however, it should be tailored to the specific family's own concerns and their cognitive abilities. Here is an explanation that the clinician might have given to the parent of the boy with the medical complications seen for projectile vomiting, as described in Chapter 2 and Figure 1.

> It is understandable that Earl's vomiting is worrisome for you, and I agree that it is important for us to find a way to eliminate or at least decrease it. While I might occasionally see him vomiting in clinic, it is difficult for me to fully understand the nature of the problem, its severity, and how it fits into your natural environment unless I were to follow him around for a week or two. Because this is not feasible, I will have to rely on you to observe for me so that I can get a detailed picture of what happens. You've given me some very useful observations in this interview, but it is difficult for me to get a full picture by only your telling me what you remember from the times he has vomited.
>
> So, I am going to ask you to keep a detailed record of every instance when Earl vomits and the circumstances surrounding these episodes. This will be very useful in looking for patterns that may tell us why this behavior occurs. After we have looked at this information together, we will decide on a treatment that fits with the information we have obtained.
>
> Then I will be asking you to continue keeping track of his vomiting and perhaps some other information we agree upon. This ongoing and repeated information is important for us to detect whether the vomiting is improving or whether we need to change our treatment.

The exact wording must be adjusted to fit the individual child or parent, but the crucial thing is that he or she sees the legitimacy of needing to get a "picture" of what goes on in the environment where the behavior exists and where it must be changed. In the clinician's initial assessment, this can be described as just "getting a picture," but ultimately he or she will want to use some such term as "getting an ongoing picture," to reflect the need for continuous monitoring of progress.

In the above example, note that the clinician acknowledged the parent's concerns, explained why data collection was necessary for devising a treatment plan, and indicated that ongoing collection of quantitative data would be a part of treatment. Note also that the clinician did not set the parent up to expect that intervention would necessarily *eliminate* the vomiting. This was important in this particular case because the etiology of the vomiting was unknown in this medically fragile child. In fact, vomiting was *not* eliminated at times when he had medical complications or new medications or formulas. It *was*, however, eliminated at those times when he was leaving the house or asked to do an unpleasant or difficult task. Without this early explanation, the clinician's credibility might have been seriously damaged or the parent might have ended treatment after the vomiting had been reduced, not recognizing that the tremendous gains she and her son had made were all that were possible.

It is advisable to ask the parent or child to tell in their own words what he or she sees as the reason for getting quantitative information. This demonstrates to the clinician that the person has understood and allows him or her opportunity to reinforce, correct, or augment that understanding. It also makes the intended data collector less likely to dispense with the data-recording tasks with a thought such as "This isn't important; it isn't what I'm going to this clinician for." Repeating back information is particularly important for children and adolescents, as well as for parents with limited cognitive skills.

4. Involve the Child and Family in Devising the Exact Procedures

Work out the precise nature of the tasks in collaboration with the child and family. They should be involved, at some level, in decision making about collecting data, including decisions on which behaviors to record, details of how to record, where to keep the materials, techniques for graphing, interpretation of the graphed data, and so on. The clinician should expect to have to educate children and families—who are usually unfamiliar with the collection and use of data—so that they can contribute to such decisions. To keep the decisions realistic, the child or parent should discuss the logistics of actually carrying out the procedures, and whenever possible practice doing so in clinic.

Discussions of data collection might even include a "brain-storming" style of problem solving, in which the parent and clinician generate alternative ways to get the clinical information and the advantages and disadvantages of each. Eventually, they should agree on a method that takes into account both cost (convenience, time, materials, embarrassment, etc.) and effectiveness (quality and quantity of data obtained). The clinician should be flexible during decision making, yet firm regarding certain issues, especially getting credible and sensitive data and the family's compliance with the decisions made. If a parent or adolescent is reluctant to implement a method the clinician thinks would be useful, either the procedure should be adjusted or the clinician should provide a more carefully reasoned argument; the clinician should not simply discount the parent's or adolescent's reluctance as ignorance or resistance.

Ultimately, success in data collection—like success in treatment—will depend on the willingness of the child and/or family to perform the necessary behaviors. This is more likely to occur if the clinician responds to the their input as valuable and reinforces their involvement. As treatment proceeds, it is important to be responsive to problems with the data-collection procedures, but firm in handling repeated failures to keep adequate records. Failure to address difficulties with data collection can inadvertently reinforce poor compliance and undermine the implementation of the therapeutic recommendations made.

5. Use Simple Procedures

Using simple procedures is helpful in engaging the child or parent in data collection. In many clinics, near the end of the very first session, the family is routinely given a data sheet to complete at home as part of the initial assessment. This necessarily will take different forms, depending upon the identified problem. In one clinic, for instance, if families are vague about the presenting problem, they are given a blank calendar sheet and asked to make a note each day about three good things that happened that day and one thing that did not work out well. In this way, not only does the therapist gain useful information for further assessment, but the family learns the clinic's emphasis on data collection from the very beginning. It is much harder to establish a pattern of collecting data after adolescents or families get accustomed to not collecting data.

Part of keeping the recording simple is not trying to record every behavior that may become a target for intervention or every environmental event that may prove important. Prioritize the behaviors and events, then select the one, two, or three that seem most important and feasible to measure at the moment. They might be "important" because they are likely to be slow to change, dangerous, very infrequent, or highly variable from day to day (which makes the typical impressionistic assessment especially unlikely to be a sensitive index of progress). Or, a clinician may give top priority to a parent or teacher behavior because it is likely to revert to its previous frequency if the parents or teachers are not held accountable by having them (or a child, spouse, colleague, etc.) measure what they are doing daily.

It is not necessary to record every instance of a behavior. Factors that should influence a decision about how much of it to record include the frequency of the behavior, how salient ("noticeable") the behavior will be when it occurs, and how motivated and "self-controlled" the observer is. For example, one child may be aggressive toward others one or two times per day, on the average, making it necessary to record each occurrence of the behavior for adequate accuracy. Another child may be aggressive so often that measuring every instance throughout the day is out of the question.

For behaviors that occur quite often, one solution is to agree upon a time period (observation session) each day—or at least several days each week—during which data will be collected. This should be a time that is sufficiently convenient for the observer, easy for him or her to remember (e.g., because he or she always does another specific thing at that time), not so lengthy as to discourage participation, and a time during which the behavior is likely to occur with sufficient frequency.

Sometimes even the frequency of opportunities for a behavior can be controlled. For example, if the behavior of interest is a child's compliance, the clinician should recognize that it is hard for the parent to detect and record all of the times (opportunities) when the child *could* comply, and this makes it difficult to determine what percent of these opportunities did result in compliance. The clinician and parent could generate a list of possible commands and requests from which the parent selects, say, four appropriate ones to give each day. The therapist has thus created such effective cuing that it should be easy for the parent to record both the command and the child's compliance/noncompliance.

Another way of recording compliance in a more controlled manner is to ask the parent to record compliance with the first five commands given each day (or at some other time of day, such as meal preparation time). Yet another way is to ask the parent to set up a 5-minute period in which they give 2–3 commands per minute, just as one might do in clinic. Recording for this short session can be quite easy if an appropriate data form is given. For example, the parent can use Form 1 (Generic Vertical Form) from the Appendix, dividing it into two columns, one labeled "Complies" (within 5 seconds of the command) and one labeled "Noncomplies." The parent puts a tally mark in the appropriate column following each command. In a two-parent family—or where there is an older child who can assist—it may be a good idea, at least initially, to have one parent give commands and the other record. Form 10 (Four Behaviors Weekly: Index Card) can also be adapted easily by writing in "Complies" and "Noncomplies" as the behaviors to be recorded in the first two rows.

Interval recording is another technique that can reduce the data collector's task. For example, if the target behavior is decreasing arguing between siblings, Form 21 (Interval Recording Weekly: Index Card) can be used to record simply "yes" (+) or "no" (−) for every hour, indicating whether the siblings did or did not interact during that 1-hour interval, and circling the "yes" if any of their interactions included arguing. The percent of *interaction intervals* that also contained *arguing* could then be calculated. This would be much easier than a frequency count. Form 20 (Scatterplot) could be used instead, if the clinician wanted information every half-hour and/or wanted to look for patterns across weeks.

Momentary time sampling can also simplify recording some behaviors. For example, suppose the behavior of interest is "play with peers" in an overly dependent, socially inept child. The parents could set a kitchen timer to go off every hour and, when it went off, record whether or not peers were present (opportunity) and whether the child was playing with any of them at that moment (behavior). Form 21 (Interval Recording Weekly: Index Card) would be particularly useful for this, given its ability to accommodate up to four behaviors. See Chapters 3 and 9 for more examples of interval recording and momentary time sampling.

Another strategy for simplifying data collection is to use portable devices, which are discussed in Chapter 3. This will increase the likelihood that the child or parent will actually record in the natural environment. Often, the device needs to be somewhat unobtrusive to save the adolescents or parents from embarrassing questions, yet sufficiently salient to remind them to record. An index card like

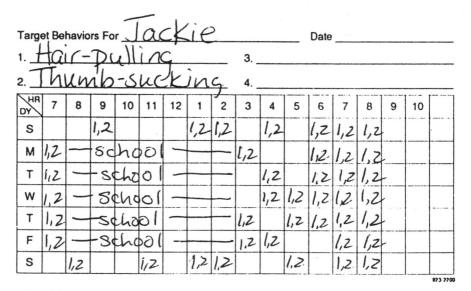

Figure 27. Interval recording of hairpulling and thumbsucking. (Form 21 in Appendix.) *Comments:* The parents were asked to record whether either of the two behaviors occurred any time during the 1-hour interval. They noted times the child was in school and consequently not observed. Based on these data, the clinician could see time patterns (evening) and co-occurrence of the two behaviors.

those depicted in Figure 2 (Form 10) and Figure 27 (Form 21) can be carried in a pocket all day; however, notice that Form 10 is most appropriate for infrequently occurring behaviors.

Form 21 can be used for 1-hour interval recording, but it can also be used for frequency recording, with the tally marks entered in the hour when the behavior occurred (or at least began). In Figure 27, parents were asked to mark whether hairpulling or thumbsucking occurred during each hour interval. One pattern noted from these data was that the two behaviors usually occurred together and that they occurred most consistently in the evening and early morning. (Sometimes there is an advantage of knowing not only how many times the behavior occurred but also when it occurred, because this can give hints about environmental and biological circumstances that are influencing the behavior.)

6. Teach the Child and Parents to Carry out the Tasks of Data Collection

Although it may seem very simple to make a mark on a form every time a certain event happens, for most clients such a task is unfamiliar and may be daunting. For any client, it is certainly not something they already do regularly. Therefore, it is important to train the relevant family members in the data-collection behaviors they have agreed to exhibit. This training should probably include the following seven steps, unless there is strong evidence that a step can be bypassed:

1 | Remind the child or parent of the *rationales* for getting quantitative information.
2 | Illustrate how this information can help by showing a *graph* of a past case and explaining what the data tell about the behavior, at a few specific points, and how that helped.
3 | *Describe* what they have agreed they are going to do (how, when, for how long, and in what circumstances the data collection is to occur).
4 | With the person's help, *generate explicit definitions* and examples of the behaviors and, if relevant, what constitutes an "opportunity" for each.
5 | *Demonstrate* appropriate use of the recording form and/or device, with either a description or, better, a role-playing of the behaviors to be recorded.
6 | Have the child or parent *practice* the recording in the office, using as lifelike situations as possible, even if only in their imagination.
7 | Have the child or parents *reiterate* accurately *what they are going to do and when*, between now and the next contact, to get the data and *what will remind them*.

7. Get a Firm Commitment to Carry out the Tasks

In some cases it is wise to get a commitment in writing. Research has shown that a combination of both oral and written agreements results in more compliance with an assigned task than an oral agreement alone, although an oral agreement produces more compliance than no explicit agreement at all (Levy, 1977). It has also been shown that a written contract outlining the nature of the task and the performance criterion results in more compliance than only an implicit commitment (Kanfer, Cox, Greiner, & Karoly, 1974).

Another procedure that may be useful for some families who are at high risk for noncompliance is to get a refundable monetary deposit. The deposit, or part of it, would be refunded contingent upon return of data at each session. This technique has been found to be effective for self-monitored data collection (Ersner-Hershfield, Connors, & Maisto, 1981). It should be accompanied by careful inquiry, since money can be a strong incentive to fill in the blanks five minutes before the beginning of a session, which would defeat the purpose of data collection. Because a new deposit will be collected at the end of the session, it may seem silly to return all or part of the deposit when the client provides credible data, but it is still a good idea to go through the process of returning the money so that an actual exchange is experienced each time the data are provided, not merely a conceptual exchange. A series of postdated checks that can be returned uncashed individually at each session is another alternative where no actual money changes hands unless the client breaks the contract.

When a client seems not to understand fully or be motivated enough to follow through on the detailed data-collection assignment, it can help to give the assignment in gradually increasing steps. The clinician can first ask the child or parent to comply with a small task—such as recording information on only one day, for only one behavior, or for only 10 minutes as soon as they get home—and then report their success, either by an immediate telephone call or at their next appointment. If the client completes this task correctly, he or she should be rewarded for doing so and then be assigned a somewhat closer approximation to the full task. If a client is rewarded for complying with a small request, he or she is more likely to comply with subsequent larger tasks (Shelton & Levy, 1981). Be aware of the strengths and limitations of individuals; set realistic subtasks so that they are likely to succeed.

MAINTAIN RECORDING BY FAMILY MEMBERS

Any effortful behavior requires cues (antecedents) and consequences that will maintain it. This is why we have been mentioning the need to reinforce data collection, just as a clinician would reinforce any compliance. It is important that reinforcement be sufficient to outweigh the "costs"—in terms of effort, embarrassment, or inconvenience—involved in the data collection. Usually, beginning each session by asking to see the information collected, immediately graphing and discussing the data, and giving some words of appreciation or admiration will suffice. In some cases, the monetary exchange already described may be necessary.

Significant others in the child's environment can undermine data collection very easily, but they can also be enlisted to help. Their role can be both to cue and reinforce compliance. These persons often control more effective reinforcers than the clinician does and they are more likely to be nearby when the child or parent should or does collect the information, so that their prompts will be timely and their reinforcement immediate. Especially in the case of a child data collector, it may be useful to have a contract between the child and a significant other that specifies contingencies of reinforcement for data collection. For example, the contract may state that the child will receive 50 cents each time he or she completes a day's data collection correctly and that the money will be put into a fund for a trip, a movie, or some other special event. A strategy more likely to be useful with parents is to have them reinforce their own data collection, such as taking a 15-minute relaxation break after a data collection period; however, such self-reinforcement occasionally must be "backed up" with other sources of reinforcement if it is to remain effective. Due to their tendency to have difficulty delaying gratification, adolescents may be less likely to withhold reinforcement if they have not collected data, thereby undermining the strategy.

Telephone calls can also be used between sessions. These can not only convince the parents that their role is essential in collecting information, but can also give the clinician the opportunity to deliver social reinforcers to them in their natural setting. By working out a schedule showing when data collection is most likely to occur, the clinician's prompts or reinforcers can be especially well timed. Alternatively, the child or parent can carry the responsibility of calling the clinician's office when he or she completes a particular assignment, leaving the data on an answering machine or voice mail.

A final consequence is the holding of a treatment session. Treatment sessions can be canceled or shortened when a data collector fails to do as he or she has agreed. However, this should be done only as a last resort and if determined to be critical to treatment. Sometimes barriers to data collection are insurmountable for children or parents, yet they continue to follow through with treatment recommendations. If they can demonstrate—either in the clinical setting or on a home visit—that therapeutic progress is genuinely occurring, it becomes less essential for them to get data daily.

For instance, suppose that on weekly clinic visits a child demonstrates greater and greater compliance from session to session. The clinician may be unsure whether the child is simply learning to comply while in clinic. But, if the parent also demonstrates better and better fluency at child management skills across these session, it may be unnecessary to have data from home on either the parent's or the child's behavior. On the other hand, if there are no clear-cut changes in the child's behavior in clinic, it is doubtful that the treatment recommendations are being followed at home. If the clinician feels that everything within his or her ability has been tried to improve follow-through at home, the most ethical course may be to refer the family to another therapist. Of course, such a decision should be discussed with the family in a way that is not belittling or disapproving.

SUMMARY

To reiterate the main points of this chapter, the following is suggested:

1. Establish rapport, making the clinician influential with the child and parent; then
2. Reach a therapeutic alliance regarding collection of quantitative clinical information by
   a. being committed to and enthusiastic about information,
   b. being prepared in advance,
   c. providing rationales that the child and parent can understand, appreciate, and preferably repeat,
   d. involving the intended data collector in deciding the exact procedures,
   e. using simple procedures,
   f. teaching the family to carry out the tasks of data collection, and
   g. getting a firm commitment to carry out the tasks.
3. Be sure the cues and consequences in the natural environment and from the clinician are adequate to maintain the client's data recording throughout treatment. The feedback from the clinician should include:
   a. beginning each session by looking at the data and discussing them,
   b. graphing and discussing the data with the child and parents immediately, and
   c. through words and facial expressions, showing admiration and appreciation of the data collector's work.

7

Interpreting Data

One of the main purposes of collecting data is so that *objective* information can influence the clinician's and family's decisions. To display them in a way that will have the most influence, the data should be graphed as soon as possible. Once the data are graphed, the graphs should be interpreted. Decisions about whether to continue a treatment, modify it in some minor way, or adopt a totally different strategy should be influenced by these interpretations of the graphed data, not by client impressions alone. Eventually, interpretations should also indicate when it is time to end a treatment.

CHARACTERISTICS TO LOOK FOR IN THE DATA

In examining a graph, clinicians should be looking for trends, stability of data, and unusual changes in behavior. Each provides important information.

Trends in Behavior

Trends are the general direction that the data are taking, and they indicate whether the behavior is generally improving, staying stable, or deteriorating. To see trends, one must look beyond the day-to-day ups and downs in the data.

Illustration: Wearing Splints

Let us illustrate with the case of Tim, a 4-year-old with juvenile rheumatoid arthritis who refused to wear his needed arm splints. His 12-year-old brother Lannie was the data collector. Lannie set a timer for various durations each day so that it went off at 10 times that were unpredictable to Tim. When it went off, Lannie would check Tim to see if he had his splints on (momentary time sampling). If Tim did, Lannie put a star on a chart kept in a little notebook and showed it to Tim. When—and *only* when—Tim had six stars (this was increased when he reached two consecutive days of 70%), he got his choice of an ice cream bar, a cookie, or a favorite fruit drink. He was not allowed desserts at other times, of course.

Figure 28 shows Lannie's data on Tim for for one baseline day and 13 days of intervention. Because days 11, 12, and 13 were disappointing, Tim's father suggested they change the intervention; he said, "It isn't working any more." But when the clinician and the father graphed the data on April 20, they could see that the first 10 days showed a strong upward trend, representing a rapid improvement in Tim's behavior. To emphasize this, the clinician took an average of days 1 through 3, an average of days 4 through 6, and an average of days 7 through 10, entering those averages with small black dots on the graph and drawing a dashed data line between them, as can be seen in Figure 29. Looking at the strong slope of improvement demonstrated by those averages, the father agreed that he had become discouraged too rapidly and the same intervention was continued. Tim's splint-wearing soon resumed its improvement and reached 100% 2 weeks later (not shown in Figure 29).

Illustration: Anna's Outbursts

Tim's case illustrates the fact that without knowing the trend, one might well discontinue an effective intervention prematurely. However, it is also easy to continue an ineffective intervention too long because of not attending to the trend. Take the case of Anna, a 13-year-old whose frequent temper outbursts were problematic in the family. Figure 30 shows data on Anna's outbursts, collected by whichever parent noticed them and could most readily record the incident. The recordings consisted of simple, small tally marks on the calendar that the family kept in the kitchen, plus occasional notes regarding what seemed to set off the outburst. In this case, the parents first collected baseline data for a week while they continued to handle the outbursts as they always had—sometimes punishing Anna by taking away a privilege, sometimes arguing with her, and sometimes trying to accommodate her in some way.

The intervention was begun on August 8, and consisted of on-the-spot, very calm, and supportive questioning of Anna about what upset her, followed by correction of any misinterpretations involved and, often, by making adjustments to accommodate Anna. The parents no longer punished Anna for her outbursts but, instead, tried to see things from her perspective, a very sensible and humane approach. These parents felt they better understood Anna as a result of such discussions. Also, as Figure 30 shows, the immediate effect of the intervention was a substantial reduction in the number of outbursts, with only one on 2 days of the first week of intervention. This pleased the parents and they felt they were on the road to a happier family.

The favorable impression continued through the next 2 weeks as well. Anna's outbursts did not cease entirely, but they seemed more tolerable, perhaps

NAME: __Tim__ MONTH: __April__ OBSERVER: __Lannie__

BEHAVIOR(S): __SPLINTS ON (+) or OFF (∅)__

DATE	1	2	3	4	5	6	7	8	9	10	TOTAL +	COMMENTS
4/7	0	0	0	0	0	0	0	0	0	0	0	
4/8	+	0	0	0	0	0	0	0	0	0	1	He got mad when I checked.
4/9	+	+	0	0	0	0	0	0	0	0	3	
4/10	0	+	+	0	0	+	0	0	0	0	3	
4/11	+	+	0	+	+	+	0	0	0	+	6	He seems to start the day well
4/12	+	+	0	0	0	0	+	0	0	0	4	
4/13	+	+	+	+	+	0	+	+	+	0	7	
4/14	0	+	+	+	+	0	0	+	+	0	8	
4/15	+	+	+	+	+	+	+	+	+	0	8	
4/16	+	+	0	+	+	+	+	+	0	0	7	
4/17	+	+	+	+	0	+	0	+	0	0	8	Mom says he may be coming down with a cold
4/18	0	0	+	0	0	0	+	0	+	+	5	He has a cold
4/19	+	+	+	0	+	+	+	0	0	0	6	
4/20	+	0	0	0	0	+	+	+	0	0	4	He's cranky today!
TOTAL												

Figure 28. Number of intervals with splints on and off. (Form 4 in Appendix.) *Comments:* Tim's brother checked on whether he was wearing his splints whenever the timer went off (at 10 random intervals), and jotted down a symbol for "on" (+) or "off" (−). These were totaled for each day in the last two columns.

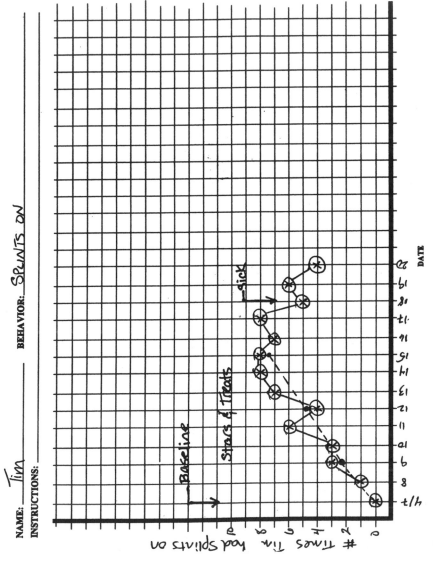

Figure 29. Graph of intervals of splint-wearing, with trend lines. (Form 6 in Appendix.) *Comments:* This is a graph of the data in Figure 28. A trend was determined by averaging each successive 3 days of data across the first 9 days, plotting the points, and connecting thems with a dashed trend line.

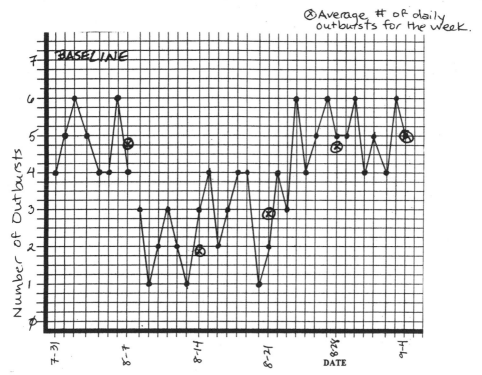

Figure 30. Frequency of outbursts per day and average number per week. (Form 7 in Appendix.) *Comments:* This is a simple polygon graph. Note that the average number of outbursts per week was graphed due to the variability of the behavior from day to day.

because the parents had a consistent way to react to them. However, by the fourth week of intervention, the parents began to doubt that they were making progress, and they raised this question to the clinician. The clinician then calculated the average number of outbursts per day for each of the 4 weeks that the parents had been attempting their intervention. Each average is shown as a circled "X" in Figure 30.

The first week of intervention achieved a mean daily rate of only 2.3 outbursts, a considerable improvement over the 4.8 per day during baseline. Although this daily mean rose to 2.9 in the second week, this was still substantially lower than the baseline mean. However, in the third week, the mean rose to 4.7, and in the fourth week to 5.0. There was a definite upward trend, and it was clear that the intervention—at least as it was being implemented—was not having a lasting beneficial effect. Either a total change of strategyor some kind of adjustment to the existing intervention was needed . If the clinician and parents had not collected and graphed the data, the parents might have simply dropped out of treatment in discouragement by the fifth or sixth week of intervention, when the treatment was not working; and the clinician might have never known why.

Ways to Evaluate Trend

To determine a trend, at least three data points are needed, although five or more is better. When there are enough data points, it is good to evaluate the trend in the data to see whether the behavior is headed in the right direction. While there are statistical formulas for determining the trend line, it is usually adequate to do one of the following:

1	Simply draw an approximate "line of best fit" (a straight line that minimizes its average distance from all the data points it passes) that, visually, seems to represent the direction the data are taking.
2	Take the average of the first half of the data points and the last half. Usually, the best average to use is a mean, but a median may be best if there are some very deviant data points. These averages can be plotted and a line drawn between, as was done in Figure 28.
3	Take an average, every week (or other time period), of the several days of data and plot these data, as was done in Figure 29. The slope of these data will tell you the trend.

If the analysis of the trend shows the data to be headed in the desired direction and at an acceptable speed, it is best to continue treatment with no changes. If the trend is opposite to the desired direction, immediately consider how best to change the intervention. If the data show no change in the behavior despite the intervention having been in effect long enough to produce change normally—again, the intervention needs to be revised.

Behavioral Stability

One of the trends we have mentioned is "no change," or behavioral stability. Once a treatment goal has been reached the behavior should be maintained long enough to assure that it will persist—that is, it should remain stable. While monitoring its stability, the clinician should also be taking steps to get the behavior change to generalize to other settings, people, or tasks. It is also often necessary to arrange for the behavioral improvement to generalize to other, similar behaviors. This usually requires systematic planning (Baer, 1981; Stokes & Baer, 1977).

Ultimately, it is necessary to reduce any artificial aspects of the treatment—aspects that are not meant to be permanent once the therapist is no longer involved—while continuing to measure the behavior and graph the data. If the improved behavior is maintained despite having "faded out" the special, temporary aspects of the intervention, then one can be reasonably confident that a lasting clinical effect has been achieved. If the behavior begins to revert to its preintervention state, the clinician should immediately consider ways that the natural environment can be permanently altered in order to maintain the desirable level of behavior.

Unusual or Sudden Changes in Behavior

Sometimes a behavior is changing in the desired direction and suddenly reverses back in the undesirable direction: the child has a setback. At that time, it is necessary to consider whether there are environmental or health factors that may be causing the setback, such as illness, a change in certain significant persons in the child's life, a threat of some significant change such as an impending move, or an accident of some kind. Do not assume that the intervention should be immediately changed, but do determine whether the child needs some form of reassurance or support. Usually a change in intervention is needed only if the setback persists for several days.

When a setback occurs, it sometimes just means that the child is "testing" whether the adults in his or her life are actually going to stick to some new way that the clinician has taught them to behave—whether they will really follow through with what the clinician has taught them. Obviously, it is essential that the adults calmly persist with the intervention, applying it with great fidelity and providing any relevant explanations to the child.

If setbacks occur repeatedly, search for any unique characteristics about the times when they occur. Often, some pattern that explains the setback can be discovered and the environment arranged in such a way that the setbacks are minimized or they have minimal detrimental effects. For example, an adolescent may become particularly noncompliant or emotional when experiencing a headache or during a menstrual cycle. Similarly, a child may become aggressive only on the days that a substitute teacher is in class, when sleep patterns are disturbed, or when the normal routine at home has been broken.

There are several types of solution to such problems: treat the medical condition, reduce expectations at those "difficult" times, or, especially, increase the supports provided for appropriate behavior. These types of solution can also be combined. It is not a good idea to forego the intervention on these difficult days, since that would teach the child to have difficult days in order to get the intervention dropped, but other things can be changed. The tasks assigned to the child can be minimized, extra help can be provided, special "rest breaks" might be added or a special friend brought in as support, and extra rewards can be given for appropriate behavior on such days.

CONCLUSION

It is clear, then, that data collection can help both the clinician and parent to understand the child's behavior and make informed decisions about treatment. Most clinicians have had the experience of the exasperated parent reporting that "Everything has gone to pieces and the program does not work." Of course this can be a result of the parents' failure to implement the program with fidelity, so the clinician's first reaction should be to test this. At other times, parents are responding to a brief setback, which can be especially disheartening when all seemed to be improving. By showing them a graph of the favorable trend in their child's behavior, the clinician can both allay their fears that the intervention is not really working and help them discover what may be causing the setbacks. Often they will, as a result, learn more about how their own behavior affects their child's behavior.

At the same time, graphs that show *consistent* worsening of the target behavior should prompt the clinician to make changes quickly, so that parents do not become discouraged and drop out before favorable outcomes can be achieved.

Troubleshooting the Problems

Even when the clinician and the child or parents all seem to be committed to collecting and using quantitative clinical information, problems can arise. We will discuss the most common ones we have encountered and the solutions we have found useful. Most of these solutions are elaborations of ideas presented in Chapter 7. Individual clinicians are encouraged to generate other possible solutions.

PROBLEM: ADULT FAILS TO COLLECT THE CLINICAL INFORMATION

This is probably the most common problem. It can be avoided, in most cases, by taking sufficient preventive steps, but because those steps can be time consuming and sometimes unnecessary, they are often bypassed, resulting in failure to collect data. There are several things that can be done to solve this problem, but the first is to see what reasons the intended data collector gives for not collecting the information.

Sometimes the person can identify the source of the problem, which is very helpful for the clinician in solving it efficiently. For example, there might be something about the behavior or situation that the clinician did not understand initially, so the system devised for collecting the data was inapplicable: it didn't fit and another system needs to be devised. Or perhaps the child had been visiting a relative, making it difficult for the parent to collect data or to get someone else to do so.

But, in many cases, the problem of failure to collect data is not straightforward, and steps are needed to motivate and teach the child or parents. The following are some suggestions.

Practice to Fluency

For most data collection, it is important to have the person practice at least a little bit in clinic, so they develop some degree of fluency at the task. Sometimes simulations of real situations can be set up, with all of the necessary persons present and engaging in the very behavior to be recorded. The data collector then performs the same data-recording behavior he or she will perform outside of the clinic. For instance, in the example of an adolescent girl with diabetes, described on page 104, the clinician had the girl test her own blood in clinic and record all relevant information agreed upon. This reassured the clinician that lack of recording was not due to a skill deficit.

Sometimes these practice simulations or "role-plays" also reveal questions or problems that a clinician might not have anticipated, and give him or her a chance to work out procedural details with the data collector that might not otherwise have been addressed. A good example of this is asking parents to record child compliance, for which they may not have a clear definition. For example, the parents may have recorded a response as "compliant" even though they had repeated the request multiple times. Or, they may be unclear how to record their observations directly on the form. By doing a 5-minute observation with the parents and providing feedback, the clinician will be more confident in the parents' ability to follow through on data collection.

At other times, it may be impossible to create a simulated situation, and it may be necessary to settle for having the parent imagine the situation. Ask them to describe real situations that have occurred, so that what they are visualizing is at least realistic and relevant. Have them actually engage in the data recording when the scene is described. Even though this may seem quite unnecessary and artificial there is the risk that the data recording may not occur reliably when such a scene occurs in daily life, if it is not done.

Have the parents practice recording many scenarios, so that they have practiced in a variety of likely situations. For example, scenarios should include various forms that the behavior might take, "borderline" instances, and various environmental situations in which the behavior might occur. Again, this is to assure that their data recording is reliably evoked by the appropriate situations in their daily life.

Here is an example where a situation would be quite difficult to simulate. The parents of a 10-year-old boy with Tourette's Syndrome wanted to record their son's tic behavior unobtrusively when in novel situations around groups of people. The clinician made a list of situations (e.g., in a grocery store, at a family barbecue, attending a school carnival). The parents were asked to visualize the setting and people and to describe them in detail. For each situation, then, the parents and clinician discussed specific ways to record the behavior without drawing attention to their son. These techniques were tried out, modified, and then practiced in clinic. The most successful technique they found was to use pennies as frequency counts. They observed in 5-minute blocks ("sessions"), usually recording for only one block during any particular activity, depending on the logistics and length of the activity. During that 5-minute observation, one designated parent transferred pennies from one pocket to the other each time their son exhibited a tic. Pennies were counted after the activity and the total recorded on a simple index card.

Although clinicians cannot expect a child or parent to record with the accuracy of a trained researcher, they need to continue practicing until it seems that the data collected will represent the behavior's status adequately for clinical purposes. This probably requires anywhere from 3 to 25 practice trials, depending on the difficulty of the data recording and the person's intellectual skills. Practicing is best continued until—across at least 3 or 4 trials and with no prompts—the data collector immediately and accurately records when the behavior of interest occurs. Time constraints may not afford the luxury of as many practice trials as seems ideal, but even one is better than none.

Contract for Quantitative Clinical Information

One way both to convince adolescents or parents that the clinician is serious and to motivate their following through is to get written commitments—commitments that involve consequences. For example, a contract with the data collector could say that he or she agrees to collect the data daily, as instructed, and that when they do so, the clinician agrees to review these data, graph them, and work with the client on his or her clinical problem. This would mean that if the person fails to collect and bring the data, the session would either be canceled or shortened by, say, 10 or 15 minutes. (It might be wise to write in some degree of flexibility, such as "forgets to bring the data more than once in five sessions.") Also, such contracting is a sensible technique only if the treatment sessions are important to the person. In fact, an opposite approach may be more appropriate with some clients. For example, with adolescents who are anxious to get on with their after-school activities, sessions might actually be shortened as *reinforcement* for collecting data.

If the clinician is not sure the sessions are important enough to the adolescent or parents, it would be advisable to come up with some other reinforcer that they get only when they have performed their data collection and other responsibilities. These need not be big reinforcers; often just some tangible recognition is sufficient. For example, one could have a chart in the child's folder where all of his or her responsibilities for the week are listed and then check off each as it has been performed. These could then be transferred to a polygon graph, with the number of tasks recorded (or the number of days of the week when the behavior was recorded) along the ordinate. It would be a good idea to have two copies of the list of tasks, one for the adolescent or parent and one for the clinician.

Change to Telephone Data-Reporting

One problem with any task that must be carried out for a whole week before one gets a reinforcer (or other feedback) is that it involves a huge delay between the behavior and the consequence. This greatly diminishes the effects of the consequence on the behavior. Thus, one solution is to have the data collector telephone the information to the clinician or to a clerk daily. Although he or she could leave the data on voice mail, it is more promising to report the data directly to a person, because that person's reinforcing reaction (it should be more than a perfunctory "Okay, thanks") is important for maintaining the behaviors of data collecting and reporting.

Set Graduated Goals

If the parents have been asked to record more than one behavior or to record throughout every day, one way to get better compliance is to reduce that task temporarily and then work up to the full task in steps. For example, a single parent brought his 6-year-old daughter into a clinic because she was "doing mean things to her 2-year-old brother." During treatment, the therapist had asked the father to record the following: (a) the frequency of the girl's aggressing toward her younger sibling; (b) the time he starts and ends each of two daily special playtimes with the girl (so the clinician can determine if the father is doing the playtimes and for how long); (c) the first five positive things he says to the girl each day; and (d) the times that he says these things.

Although not an unreasonable list of data-recording tasks, it proved to be more than the father was able to manage all at once. To remedy this problem, the clinician told the father that, although he would need to record all of this information eventually, for now he need only record the aggressive incidents, since those were the reason for referral and the most important outcome. When the father had done that recording faithfully for 2 weeks, the clinician added the recording of the daily play sessions. Then, 2 weeks later, she added the recording of his positive statements to the girl. If the father had found that full task still too difficult, the clinician could have had him record for just the most problematic part of the day, such as from 5:00 to 7:00, when he first got home from work.

Poor compliance with data collection should lead the therapist to question how likely it is that the client will comply with agreements or recommendations about other behavior changes and thus about treatment. Although the two are not necessarily linked, the absence of data will leave the therapist trying to decipher somewhat blindly what is or is not working. Consequently, poor data collection should be addressed directly and honestly. The therapist might want to say "I understand that keeping a record at home can be hard, but it is difficult for us to know what is or isn't working without this. Is there something we can do to make it easier for you to keep a record?" A client's repeated failure to collect data as planned should lead the clinician to analyze reasons for this and to determine if further treatment is likely to succeed.

PROBLEM: CHILD OR ADOLESCENT FAILS TO COLLECT DATA AS REQUESTED

Children who are 9 years old or more are sometimes asked to collect data, and adolescents are usually the primary data collector, both because they need to be treated as able to accept responsibilities and because having a parent collect data may set the stage for parent–adolescent conflict. Furthermore, there are some behaviors that are best recorded by the child or adolescent (for example, a SUDS rating; relaxation practices; reports of private internal events, such as flashbacks to a trauma). However, it is also common for both children and adolescents to fail to follow through for a variety of reasons that are similar to the problems parents have in collecting data.

In addition, children may not collect data because, developmentally, they are less able to see the value of the process. They may have minimal motivation to change the behaviors being targeted, making it unlikely that they will be motivated to record the behavior, or they may recognize that they have not been following through on treatment recommendations and see data as confirmation of their lack of follow-through. Finally, data collection can become a source of conflict between the child/adolescent and the parents, either in terms of compliance with keeping the data, or in terms of providing parents with ammunition for nagging.

Many of the recommendations made earlier for parents are also applicable when a child is the one collecting the data; however, there are three further recommendations. First, sometimes children show more motivation to keep data if given the choice of keeping data themselves or letting someone else do it. In some instances—such as the recording of compliance with a complicated medical regimen—it is probably best to suggest only minimal ways for the youngster to help with recording, due to the importance of accuracy. On the other hand, if recording is an important part of the regimen itself, it is a good idea to set graduated goals and teach the youngster to self-record (see example of a girl with diabetes on page 104). Our second recommendation is that, with a child, it may be especially important to set up reinforcers for data collection. Those reinforcers can be provided by the parent or by the clinician. Third, it is sometimes necessary to have a parent monitor the child's data collection and give feedback, to be sure the clinical information is collected correctly.

PROBLEM: ADOLESCENT OR PARENT LOSES DATA SHEETS AT HOME

Sometimes adolescents or parents will return to the clinic without the data and explain that they could not find the data forms. While this might be the client's way of saying that they did not record the data, it is probably best to handle the situation as a problem of disorganization. First, it is a good idea to reiterate the reasons why data are important, since data collection is not what most individuals expect when they come to a clinician. Then the clinician should try to find out where the process is breaking down. The very fact that the person could not find the forms identifies one problem: the clinician can ask where the person puts the data sheets when the clinician hands them to the person, where the sheets are when they get into their car to go home, where they are put when they arrive home, and where they are kept at home. Do any younger children have an opportunity to get hold of them at home? And so on. Even if this reiteration of the rationales for data collection and these inquiries about the data forms fail to reveal possible solutions, they at least convince the data collector that this is a significant problem, not one to just let pass.

Once the process has been broken down, the clinician should engage the data collector in problem solving about losing the forms. Here are examples of possible solutions that have been used by clinicians.

1	Keep the data forms and a pen/pencil in a brightly colored folder or envelope provided by the clinician.
2	Place the data forms in just one specific place, such as posted on the refrigerator, with a pen/pencil placed on top of the refrigerator (or attached with a string). Some clinicians collect golf pencils and give them to clients attached to the data form.
3	Keep data forms on a clipboard (with pen/pencil) that the parent will hang on a hook to be placed outside their child's bedroom, where the child's problem is occurring most often.
4	Have the data form reduced and printed on index cards, so the adolescent or parent can more easily carry them at all times. (See Form 10 and Form 21 in Appendix for examples.)
5	Have the data initially recorded in ink on the palm of the data collector's hand or on a piece of tape on the hand, instead of on the paper form. Then, at a more convenient time, the data collector can transfer these data to the form, which will always be kept in the same place.
6	Have the adolescent or parent initially count the behaviors by transferring a coin, from the righthand pocket to the left. Later, the data collector can transfer the data to the paper form.

PROBLEM: PARENT OR ADOLESCENT FORGETS TO BRING THE DATA TO THEIR APPOINTMENT

As is the case when the client reports losing the form, forgetting the data can be a legitimate problem of organization—or it can be a way to avoid telling the clinician directly that the data were not collected. Once again, it is usually best to handle the problem as one of organization. As such, the clinician should proceed in a manner similar to the approach mentioned above.

It is probably wise for the clinician to begin by expressing mild disappointment (but not irritation) that the data are not available, and then explain at length the resulting difficulty in making decisions about how to proceed with the intervention. A brief review of the rationale for data collection, as described in Chapter 2, is important, if only to convince the person that the clinician is serious. Having the data collector also restate the rationale would ensure that he or she understands. Finally, further practice of data collection in clinic can be useful.

Review does three things: (a) it reteaches the rationale and the recording procedure; (b) it convinces the data collector—far more than merely saying so—that clinician is serious about getting quantitative information and about keeping commitments in general; and (c) it gently corrects the person for irresponsible behavior by postponing the more reinforcing activity of discussing their clinical problem.

Use Prompts

Approaching the problem as one of organization should suggest the need for problem solving. One solution that might be considered is prompting, and several things can be done to prompt the data collector to bring in the data. For example, if there is telephone contact between sessions, the clinician can make a point of asking what the data are looking like and reminding the person to bring them to their session. Another prompting procedure is to arrange for the forms to be placed where the data collector must pass them every time he or she goes out the door, so that this reminds him or her to bring the data. Finally, the person may be able to get someone else's help in remembering. For instance, in the case of an adolescent data collector, it can be prearranged for a parent (who may intentionally not be involved in data- collection process) to remind the youth right before an appointment to bring the information. Similarly, a child or adolescent might play the role of reminding the parent to bring the information to appointments. If the therapist has arranged for a reinforcer in clinic based on the outcome of the data (or on merely returning data), this can be a natural motivator for the child to ensure that the clinician gets the information.

PROBLEM: DATA COLLECTOR IS ESTIMATING OR IS RECORDING DATA RIGHT BEFORE SESSIONS

Some people's data seem questionable. For example, it is sometimes fairly clear that the information was written all at one time (e.g., if the ink and spacing of data are uniform and neat), rather than each day as the behavior occurred. Sometimes the data may be just too good, given the effort that the client seems to have put into changing the behavior. Or the data may be too regular, without the normal variability one sees in behavior. Or, perhaps when asked to describe events that were recorded, the description is vague.

It is countertherapeutic to accept the client's misrepresentations. In most instances, it is best to gently remind the client that it is important to record as the behavior occurs, and repeat the rationale for doing so. If the clinician prefaces any challenge to the accuracy or timing of data collection with positive statements about any efforts the person has made, it will help the data collector accept any negative feedback as nonjudgmental.

Further probing might include asking the person at what time they recorded the data. Not only does this questioning emphasize the fact that the clinician takes data very seriously, but it may lead the person to reveal that they did, in fact, fail to follow the plan for recording immediately and according to the definitions. While it is not productive to censure the person for failing to collect the information, it is unwise to let the matter go. Perhaps the person has been hiding a reading skill deficit or misplaced the data forms until just before the appointment, in which case the suggestions provided in other sections of this chapter are applicable. Regardless, remedial action based on the nature of the problem should be taken.

The following example of an adolescent with diabetes illustrates several of the points we have made. Sharon appeared to record all of her blood glucose levels and other data for the week at one time, seemingly making up some of the data. The diabetes team had asked her to enter the glucose readings—obtained from a glucometer—four times a day in a logbook, along with insulin doses, circumstances surrounding any hypoglycemia, and any activity changes. In this way the child, parents, and physician could look at patterns indicating the need to change the girl's regimen. Without this information, it is difficult to ensure good blood sugar control. A pediatric psychologist was helping Sharon with regimen adherence and Sharon had begun testing herself more regularly, but it appeared she was not recording glucose readings in the logbook until right before her appointments, which was possible to do accurately because the glucometer stores the information. The problem with this was that all of the other information she was to record was then not entered on schedule and was of questionable validity. In fact, on one occasion, she had written in her insulin doses for dates in the future.

The therapist discussed this with Sharon by commenting, "I see a big improvement in the number of times that you are testing your blood, and I notice that your blood sugar levels were really good at Thursday noon. Can you tell me what you were doing that day at school?" "Your sugar levels were quite high on Tuesday evening. Can you tell me what you were eating or doing that might account for those highs?" Because the therapist asked for specific information about specific days, Sharon had the opportunity to experience firsthand the difficulty of recalling information without accurate records. When Sharon admitted that she could not recall her eating habits or activities, the therapist commented, "The fact that you tested was excellent because it gave you feedback right away and a chance to adjust your regimen on the spot. As you can see, however, it's pretty hard for us to see a pattern without knowing what happened at the times of these blood tests. When did you write them in your log?" Sharon then stated that she had recorded them right before the session. The therapist responded, "It's hard to remember to record them every day, but that will help us to look for patterns. Over this next week, I'd like you to do an experiment with me. The purpose of this is to determine the value of keeping records daily. For one week, I'd like to you write in your test results as you get them and your doses as you take your insulin. And very briefly write down activity or eating changes. I'm asking you to try this for just 1 week, so that we can see if it helps you to remember your regimen and so that together we can look at how to simplify things if it is too time-consuming." Sharon agreed to do this for 1 week. The following week, Sharon and the therapist discussed the log in detail and she was able to see that her recall was far better. However, she found it time-consuming to write in food and activities and was reluctant to continue the daily recording. Consequently, they together devised a simple coding system for types of food eaten and activities engaged in. The therapist contracted with Sharon to record her insulin and blood tests daily and to fill in the codes for food and activity only if blood glucose levels were unusually high or low (with these levels specified clearly). Sharon complied and the diabetes team had the information they needed.

Other forms of inquiry that might have been useful would be asking Sharon where she kept the log when at school, or how she recorded when out with friends. Visualizing situations that the adolescent describes will often invite questions about the data recording, and every question is a further message to clients that you are serious about getting credible quantitative information. The idea is not to catch clients in a lie, but rather to get them to, first, be truthful with the therapist and, second, record the data in either the manner they initially agreed to or in some planned manner that is better adapted to the situations they face.

PROBLEM: THE CHILD, ADOLESCENT, OR PARENT HAS INSUFFICIENT SKILL OR MOTIVATION

If it appears that the data collector is either not taking the task seriously enough or is just not fluent enough at the recording task, the best solution is further, more intensive practice in the clinician's presence. Be creative: do something to create a good variety of situations that resemble those the person really encounters. Maybe realism can be obtained by carrying out the training in the child's real life, or by interviewing the data collector extensively about situations that occur and the environmental contexts in which they occur. As before, the goal is for the person to do the correct recording immediately when the target behavior occurs, even when the recording form and a pen or pencil are not already in his or her hands, and several irrelevant distracting stimuli are present. As with any clinical problem, the behavior of recording must become automatic (fluent) before one can be confident that the person will show that behavior outside of clinic.

PROBLEM: THE RECORDING TASK IS DIFFICULT

It may become clear that what the clinician has asked the data collector to do is just too difficult or overwhelming for him or her to begin doing all in one step. This can be handled by breaking down the overall task into smaller tasks and getting the data collector to carry out just one or two of these smaller tasks initially. When he or she is proficient at that, add another task or two. By building up the whole job gradually, the person's success is more likely. The case example of the adolescent with diabetes exemplifies this approach.

Alternatively, the clinician may decide that the whole task is just too difficult for this person at this time, in which case it is probably a good idea to figure out a much easier way to accomplish the goal of getting an adequate measure of target-behavior performance. Perhaps instead of asking the person to measure all day, two half-hour samples would suffice. These could be samples of times of day when the target problem is especially severe or significant. Or perhaps a different recording method would be easier. For example, interval recording is easier than frequency recording, especially if intervals are an hour or more long. Perhaps the clinician can arrange for a clinic-based assessment that occurs frequently enough to provide an adequate picture of progress (as in Hembree-Kigin & McNeil, 1995) when combined with a simple form to be completed by the data collector only at the end of each day.

Finally, it is an important to remember that clinicians can underestimate the complexity of the recording task (or intervention, for that matter) or the amount of effort needed to carry out the task. Overwhelming a family member with too many or too complicated expectations is a setup for failure and for client dissatisfaction.

PROBLEM: THE CHILD, ADOLESCENT, OR PARENT READING SKILLS ARE LIMITED

Many data are to be collected on forms that include instructions or definitions. However, even some adult clients—probably more than most clinicians realize—cannot read well enough to understand such information. Two good solutions are to use pictograms instead of words, or to make the written material unnecessary by having the person who is to collect data master the skills of recording in the clinician's presence.

Use Pictograms

Figure 31 is an adaptation of what one clinician used to get a parent to record her 6-year-old child's performance of the daily routine without prompting. The clinician drew the pictures, with the child's suggestions and feedback. Although the child was learning to read, the picture prompts made it more interesting and easier to use.

Figure 32 is another example of a pictogram used with parents who had limited reading skills. The child, Chris, had a simple point system in which he received points for each of the two behaviors and four chores listed at the bottom of the page (the number of points for each was listed under the picture). Each time a point was earned, a square was immediately "X"'d out in one of the five categories of privileges, with Chris choosing which one. When all squares were filled in, Chris got the reward pictured to the right of the squares.

Practice to Fluency

If the data collector has mastered the skill of recording data at the right times, the written instructions become unnecessary. Thus, practicing, as described earlier, can be used in this circumstance as well; it may simply be necessary to have more practices so that the recording behavior becomes more automatic.

PROBLEM: THE PARENT CANNOT AFFORD SOME ITEM NEEDED FOR RECORDING

Clinicians will probably ask some families to use a stopwatch, timer, audiotape recorder, or other device in their data collection. If the parents say they cannot afford the item, it is best not to challenge the veracity of this statement, but to work with the family to discover alternative data-collection methods that require little or no money. For example, if a clinician wants parents to use a stopwatch to record how long it takes Anthony to appear at the breakfast table after he is called, the parents could merely write down the time that they called him and the time that he arrived, based on looking at a clock. Another example of this was depicted in Figure 5, in which the parents recorded duration of glasses-wearing by recording "time put on" and "time taken off" and then calculating the total number of minutes.

It is rare that expensive equipment is essential. However, if some equipment is essential—such as biofeedback devices or wet-bed alarms—probably the best solution is to loan or rent it to the family. It would be wise to come up with a plan, together with the parents, for how to prevent the item from being broken, lost, or stolen, and to discuss financial arrangements should this occur. Some clinicians require a security deposit when loaning equipment. If equipment is to be loaned, it

ANTHONY'S WEEK (9-21 to 9-27)

		Monday	Tuesday	Wednesday	Thursday	Friday	Saturday	Sunday
	A.M.							
READY FOR SCHOOL	Face / Hair / Teeth	☺	☺	—	☺	☺	X	X
ROOM CHORES	Bed	☺	☺	☺	☺	☺	☺	—
	Clean room	X	X	X	X	X	☺	X
FEED CATS		☺	☺	☺	☺	☺	☺	☺
	P.M.							
HOMEWORK DONE		☺	☺	☺	—	X	X	☺
READY FOR BED	Face / Teeth / Jammies	—	☺	☺	☺	☺	☺	☺
TRASH		X	☺	X	X	X	X	X
TOTAL FOR DAY		4/5	6/6	4/5	4/5	4/4	4/4	3/4
TIME-OUTS		ll	0̸	l	l	0̸	0̸	0̸

Figure 31. Pictogram of daily routine. (Adaptation of Form 25 in Appendix.) *Comments:* The mother used this form to give feedback to a 6-year-old child on daily routine chores. She gave the child an allowance based on reaching a criterion of 90%. Time-outs on a particular chair were noted with tally marks; happy faces were used for completing the task, and a dash was used if the task was not completed.

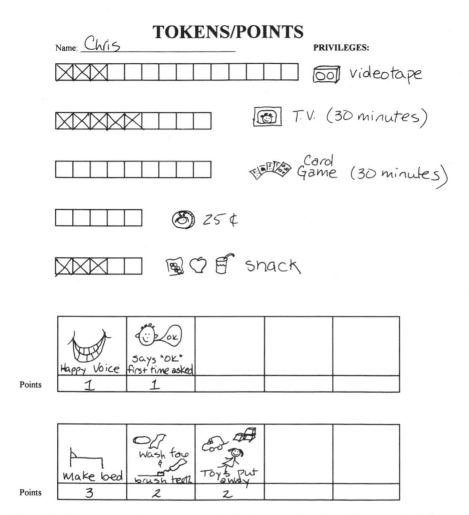

TOKENS/POINTS

Name: Chris

PRIVILEGES:

videotape

T.V. (30 minutes)

Card Game (30 minutes)

25¢

snack

Happy Voice	Says "OK" first time asked			
Points				
1	1			

Make bed	Wash face & brush teeth	Toys put away		
Points				
3	2	2		

Figure 32. Pictogram of point system combined with data collection. (Form 33 in Appendix.) *Comments:* This is a simplified chart for points (also called tokens). The clincian drew in the expected behaviors and chores and their designated points at the bottom of the page. Privileges were drawn beside lines of varying numbers of squares (each square represents one point). As Chris earned a point, a box was "X"ed next to the privilege he wanted to earn. When all the squares were filled in, he received the reward.

would also be wise to use only fairly sturdy and inexpensive devices, because some of them will definitely be lost, stolen, or broken.

CONCLUDING REMARKS

When clients fail to collect reasonable data, even after one's troubleshooting and adapting to their individual needs, you should consider what factors are contributing to this persistent problem. It is possible that failure to collect quantitative clinical information may be indicative of overall failure to follow treatment plans, although not necessarily so. Nonetheless, the therapist may need to evaluate whether, in the absence of compliance with data collection, further treatment is appropriate.

It is our hope that the reader is convinced of the value of collecting direct measures of clinical outcomes both during initial assessment and continuously throughout treatment. These data, when graphed and interpreted regularly, are a form of accountability unlike any other—accountability to the client, to oneself, to a supervisor, and/or to managed care. The process improves both the effectiveness and the efficiency of behavioral health services, just as measures of physical entities like blood pressure improve the effectiveness of medical services.

We have presented several different methods for directly measuring behavioral health outcomes and illustrated each several times. Chapter 9 presents several case examples that will provide further illustration. It is now up to the reader to put that information into practice. The manner in which data are collected and families are enticed into collecting them is only as limited as the practitioner's own imagination.

Case Illustrations

This chapter presents four cases to illustrate the role of direct and frequent measurement in treating children and their families. The cases are based on real ones or on combinations of real cases. They are somewhat simplified to avoid emphasizing details about the treatment itself, because presenting the specifics of treatment is not our purpose here. In each case we will refer to a form used to collect data; the form numbers are those given in the Appendix to this book, where blank forms are provided and may be copied or adapted as the reader wishes.

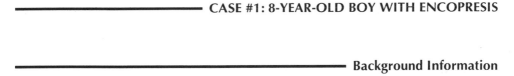

CASE #1: 8-YEAR-OLD BOY WITH ENCOPRESIS

Background Information

Donny was an 8-year-old, third-grade boy referred by his pediatrician because he soiled his pants regularly and was chronically constipated. He had two older brothers and one younger sister. His father was a blue-collar worker and his mother worked 2 days a week outside the home as well. Donny's parents rated their marriage as "good." Their home was well organized and there were clear, reasonable rules and responsibilities for the children.

The parents reported that the pregnancy for Donny was unremarkable and that he had always been a healthy child, aside from the referral problems. He was toilet trained at 2½ years of age, but then when he was 4 he became constipated after having a cold for which he took decongestant for a week.

The Child Behavior Checklist (Achenbach, 1991) and the Eyberg Child Behavior Inventory (Eyberg, 1974). showed no clinically significant scores on any subscale, and the parents reported Donny to be well behaved and cheerful overall at both home and school. His achievement had been approximately average throughout his school years and the parents reported no areas that concerned either them or Donny's teachers.

Continuous Measurement

Data Collection

Form 22 (see Appendix) was used to record Donny's soiling, any wetting of his pants, his defecation in the toilet, and the volume of the feces. The parents were also to record anything unusual about the consistency of the feces. The form was used initially in order to determine any pattern to soiling and bowel movements in the toilet. Although Form 22 was designed for recording at the end of each half-hour of the day, the parents were asked to check Donny's pants and record only once every hour, having him change his pants whenever he was found soiled.

The completed week of baseline data is shown in Figure 33. Notice the simple code at the top. Each time the parents recorded an "S" for soiled, they estimated fecal volume and consistency. At the bottom is the total number of times they found him soiled each day and the total number of occasions of defecating in the toilet. Notice that Donny's bowel movements were usually small, hard and pebblelike, which is common in children who are constipated. The pediatrician's exam confirmed this.

Form 3 was used by the parents following baseline. This required less intense recording than the form used in baseline. Initially, the parents recorded bowel movements in the toilet, size and consistency, and the number of soilings. Diet-related items were added later, as described below. See Figure 34 for these data.

Data Plotting and Analysis

Each week on a cumulative graph (Figure 35) we plotted the number of additional soilings that had occurred each day. We also plotted the number of further bowel movements in the toilet (regardless of volume), because our goal was to increase these as well as eliminate the soilings. Donny's soiling occurred one or more times each day (mean=1.7), with a consistency of hard pebbles (see Fig. 33), while his using the toilet occurred only every few days (10/1 and 10/3, also hard pebbles). Notice that, since we were adding each week's data to the data that had already accumulated, Figure 35 constitutes a cumulative record. A cumulative record is most likely to be useful when the event being recorded is infrequent. However, because understanding a cumulative record requires that one look at the *slope* of the data line, not its height, cumulative records are often hard for a novice to understand without explanation.

Functional Case Formulation

Based on the pediatrician's and parents' reports and the baseline data, Donny was showing a pattern consistent with chronic constipation. This was probably the re-

NAME: Donny DATES: 9-29 - 10-5 OBSERVER: Mom + Dad
BEHAVIOR(S): D=Dry W=Wet S=Soiled BM=BM in toilet
PANTS CHECK ON HOUR

	SUNDAY	MONDAY	TUESDAY	WEDNESDAY	THURSDAY	FRIDAY	SATURDAY
7-7:30 am	D	D	D	D	D	D	D
8:00-8:30	D	D	S (⅛c)	D	D	S	D
9:00-9:30	S (pebbles)	D	D	D	D	D	D
10:00-10:30	D	D	D	S	D	D	D
11:00-11:30	D	S (⅛c)	D	D	D	S (¼c)	D
12-12:30pm	D	D	D	D	S (pebbles)	D	S (pebbles)
1:00-1:30	S (pebbles)	D	D	S (¼c)	D	D	D
2:00-2:30	D	D	D	D	D	D	D
3:00-3:30	D	S (pebbles)	D	D	D	S (⅛c)	D
4:00-4:30	D	D	D	D	D	D	D
5:00-5:30	D	D	D	D	D	D	D
6:00-6:30	D	D	BM 1½c hard	D	D	D	D
7pm-7am	D	D	D	D	BM ¼c hard	D	D
TOTAL	S=2 BM=0	S=2 BM=0	S=1 BM=1	S=1 BM=0	S=1 BM=1	S=2 BM=0	S=1 BM=0
WEEK: TOTAL	S=12 BM=2.						

Figure 33. Case #1: 8-year-old boy with encopresis baseline data hourly record of encopresis/enuresis (Form 22 in Appendix.) *Comments:* The parents did an hourly check and recorded dry soiling, wetting, defecating in the toilet, and the volume and consistency of bowel movements. This form was selected so that the clinician could look for patterns of soiling and defecating throughout the day.

NAME: Donny   MONTH: Oct.   OBSERVER: _____

BEHAVIOR(S): BM's

DAY	BM in toilet	Size	consistency (S = soft, h = hard)	Soils	Hi Fiber # servings	# Fluids (8 oz. glasses)	COMMENTS
1							
2							
3							
4							
5							
6							
7							
8							
9	/	½c	S	1			
10	/	¼c	S	Ø			
11	/	½c	med(S)	Ø			
12	/	⅓c	h	1			b.m. harder
13	/	½c	h	Ø			
14	/	⅓c	h	Ø			
15	/	½c	h	1			
16	/	⅓c	h	Ø			
17	/	½c	med(S)	Ø			
18	/	¼c	h	1			some straining
19	/	¼c	h	1			
20	/	¼c	h	1			
21	/	¼c	h	1			*Add Fiber Fluid goals + recording
22	/	½c	h	1	3	6	
23	/	¾c	med(S)	Ø	4	7	
24	/	¾c	med(S)	1	2	5	
25	/	1c	S	Ø	3	7	
26	/	1c	S	Ø	3	6	
27	/	¾c	med(S)	Ø	2	7	
28	/	1c	S	Ø	4	6	
29	/	1c	S	Ø	3	6	
30	/	1c	S	Ø	3	7	
31	/	¾c	S	Ø	3	8	
TOTAL							

Figure 34. Case #1: 8-year-old boy with encopresis. Intervention data were a daily record of bowel movements and soilings (Form 2 in Appendix). *Comments:* The parents were asked to record the number of soilings, as well as the size and consistency of bowel movements. Note that, although Donny was having fewer soilings and defecating on the toilet regularly, the consistency was hard and the volume smaller than would be expected. Therefore, a second intervention targeting diet was implemented.

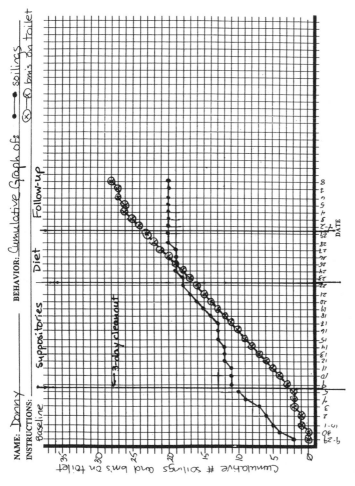

Figure 35. Case #1: 8-year-old boy with encopresis: summary graph. (Form 7 in Appendix.) *Comments:* Note that the slope for soilings is steep in baseline, levels off initially during the use of suppositories, and then begins to steepen again. This indicated to the therapist the need for an additional intervention targeting diet directly.

sult of painful defecation due to hard, overly large stools on one or more occasions when he had been taking decongestants. This resulted in his difficulty at defecating at all, which left his bowel impacted (megacolon). In turn, this led to overflow incontinence and thus soiled pants, yet great difficulty at completely evacuating. It was therefore important for a medical intervention to clean him out prior to implementing a behavioral program.

Intervention and Results

Treatment

The treatment required that, first, Donny get a thorough "cleanout" from his pediatrician, so that there was no residual hard stool in the colon. Once this was accomplished, Donny was given stool softeners at the pediatrician's suggestion, while the toilet retraining program was carried out (in continued consultation with the pediatrician). In addition, if he did not defecate on his own, he was given a glycerin suppository to ensure that his colon remained cleaned out daily. These suppositories were faded once he began using the toilet regularly.

Donny's parents were instructed to change his diet to increase his fiber and fluid intake dramatically while reducing the milk products he consumed. They were also encouraged to increase his physical activity. At least as important, the parents were to see that Donny sat on the toilet for 5 minutes daily after breakfast and if he did not have a bowel movement then, again for 5 minutes after supper. The parents were asked not to be at all negative about this, even if he did not succeed, but they were to be exceedingly positive when he did succeed.

A motivation system was devised in which Donny would get 5 points for defecating in the toilet during one of the daily "sits" or at any other time, and 5 points per day for cooperating with the high-fiber-fluid diet. In addition, he would get 5 more points if he did not soil for a day. The points were used to "buy" a privilege or material item from a "menu" of items that we, the parents, and Donny developed jointly (and revised occasionally).

Continued Data Collection

Based on difficulties described below, when intervention began we asked the parents to also collect data on high-fiber servings and fluid intake, using the data-collection form shown in Figure 34.

Treatment Results

In Figure 35, note that the data collection was discontinued for three days while the "cleanout" was underway. When data collection was resumed, Donny had a bowel movement in the toilet every day, which shows as a constantly rising data line. Also, his soilings occurred only occasionally—on days 4, 7, 12, and 20—instead of one or more times a day, as in baseline. The steep slope of baseline compared to the shallow slope during intervention reflects this great improvement. However, the volume of the bowel movements was less than desired, the consistency remained rather hard, and he continued to have occasional soilings.

In an interview with the parents and Donny, it was determined that he was having difficultly complying with the high-fiber diet, and was resisting eating vegetables, as well as foods with bran content. He complained bitterly, resulting in the parents' permitting frequent deviations from the diet. Thus we started an additional intervention.

Expanded Intervention and Data Collection

The parents were given recipes for high-fiber cookies and muffins. In addition, they were given a list of high-fiber foods. Finally, the parents bought high-fiber wafers at the pharmacy. We asked that a supply of at least three of these options be constantly available from which Donny could choose a dessert or snack as much as three times a day. He was to be allowed no other desserts. Other than that, his high-fiber diet was to remain the same. In addition, however, he was to drink eight glasses of juice or water per day, avoiding milk products. The parents agreed to always have at least one kind of fruit juice available in the refrigerator and a container of water for Donny's exclusive use, so they could measure how much he drank.

We asked the parents to record—with Donny's help, if he chose—additional data on the form illustrated in Figure 33. They were to put a tally in each day's cell for each serving of a high-fiber food Donny ate and a number indicating their estimate of the number of ounces of fluids he drank. We also expanded the motivation system so that he would be rewarded for eating and drinking these items.

Results of Expanded Intervention

The parents were very diligent about keeping a good supply of high-fiber foods on hand and usually two kinds of fruit juice. Further, Donny was greatly pleased at being allowed to eat these more appealing high-fiber foods, compared to the large helpings of vegetables he had been expected to eat earlier. As Figure 35 shows, Donny's soilings decreased with this addition to the intervention. Suppositories were faded and he continued to have bowel movements on his own.

Follow Up

Six months after the intervention was officially ended we phoned Donny's home and asked the parents to resume data collection for 1 week before coming in for their 6-month follow-up visit. They readily agreed and said that Donny would probably choose to do most of the data collection, because he was proud of his success.

As Figure 35 shows, Donny was soil-free and defecating in the toilet consistently. The parents reported that he had one relapse at about the second month after the end of treatment, at a time when the family was on vacation. After returning from vacation, the family resumed the 5-minute sits and increased Donny's fiber intake for 1 week, at which time he was back on schedule.

Also during the 6 months, the family had reduced their use of high-fiber cookies and muffins, but they did continue to expect Donny to either eat plenty of vegetables or take 2 tablespoons of bran each day. They kept juice and water available in the refrigerator at all times and Donny often drank it.

CASE #2: 14-MONTH-OLD BOY WITH SLEEP PROBLEMS

Background Information

Malik was brought in by his parents at age 14 months with the complaint of frequent awakenings at night and excessive crying. Their family physician had suggested they seek our help. He was the parents' first child and they had no plans for more. They rated their marriage as "fair." Both parents were new to the area and had moved twice since Malik was born. They both worked for the post office, but they reported having no friends in the area yet. Nor did they attend church or any other social groups.

The pregnancy for Malik had been normal. He had a history of colic, but otherwise his developmental and medical histories were typical. The family physician could find no physical cause for the awakenings. The Infant Behavior Questionnaire was administered and showed Malik to fit the pattern of a "difficult baby."

Measurement

Data Collection

Using Form 13 (Figure 36), we taught both parents how to record when Malik fell asleep and when he awakened, regardless of the time of day or night. We also asked them to write notes on the form to indicate what they did when Malik awoke, any times that Malik slept in their bed, and any other unusual situations or events that might be of interest to us.

In teaching this recording method, it took the father some time to be able to record accurately during the simulations we used, but he finally did master it. From these data we could get good estimates of the total amount of time Malik slept, the duration of the sleeping episodes, how the episodes were distributed through the day and night, and, we hoped, other events that might be relevant.

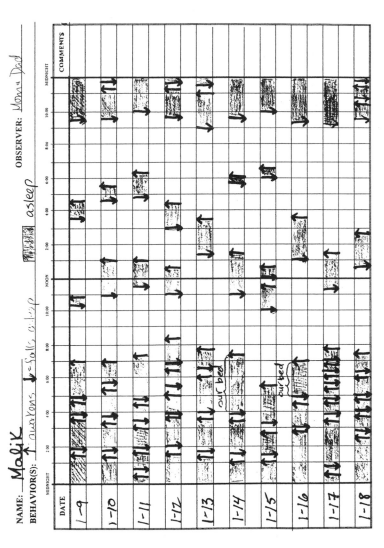

Figure 36. Case #2: Duration recording of sleep in 14-month-old boy with sleep problems. (Form 13 in Appendix.) *Comments:* The parents were asked to indicate times that Malik was taken out of bed with an upward arrow and times he was put in bed with a downward arrow, shading in times when he was asleep. They also indicated times he was taken into their bed. After baseline, they were asked to record the milk–water ratio in his bottle and to indicate scheduled awakenings with a red pen.

Data Plotting and Analysis

We summarized the data on the form in Figure 37 and plotted them on the graph in Figure 38. The parents recorded a mean of 3.5 awakenings per night. By verbal report, each time Malik awakened, he was given milk and then usually fell asleep with the mother feeding him a bottle and rocking him. On three occasions, the parents took him into their bed when he fussed in the night.

Functional Case Formulation

We hypothesized that Malik was overly dependent upon the bottle and his mother's rocking as transitional objects for sleep. When normal awakenings occurred during the night, he cried and the crying was reinforced by his mother's affectionate attention, rocking, and food. He had not developed the skill of patient, relaxed waiting to fall back asleep. Furthermore, he may have been experiencing conditioned hunger awakening due to the frequent drinking of milk in the night.

Intervention and Results

Treatment

We instructed the parents to provide a transitional object—such as a soft blanket—that would help Malik get through awakenings without relying on the parents. We also asked them to thin out his milk gradually over a 2-week period until he was receiving only water during nighttime feedings. In this way, his body could adjust to going through the night without a feeding. The bottles were then completely faded by reducing the volume each night.

The parents also agreed to schedule approximately three awakenings each night for Malik, their timing being planned to occur shortly before times that Malik had awakened during the baseline period. The times we chose with the parents were 1:45 A.M., 3:00 A.M., and 4:15 A.M.

Continued Data Collection

The parents continued the same recording.

Treatment Results

The parents reduced the milk/water ratio from the baseline of 8/0 to all water (0/8) over a 2-week period. Malik's spontaneous (unplanned) nighttime awakenings declined to a mean of 2.1 in the first week of treatment. Planned awakening times were gradually backed up in ½-hour increments such that the first awakening

NAME: __Malik__   MONTH: __Jan/Feb__   OBSERVER: _____
BEHAVIOR(S): __sleep summary data.__

DATE	# awakenings on own	# planned awakenings	milk: water	Parents took into their bed	COMMENTS
1-9	3		8:∅		Baseline
1-10	4		"		
1-11	4		"		
1-12	5		"		
1-13	4		"		
1-14	2		"	✓	
1-15	2		"		mean = 3.4
1-16	2		"	✓	
1-17	6		"		
1-18	4		"		
1-19	3		"	✓	
1-20	4		"		mean = 3.8
1-21	2	3	7:1		Treatment
1-22	3	3	"	✓	
1-23	2	3	6:2		
1-24	1	3	"	✓	
1-25	4	3	5:3		
1-26	2	3	"		
1-27	1	2	4:4		mean = 2.1
1-28	2	2	"		
1-29	2	2	3:5		
1-30	2	2	"		
2-1	∅	2	2:6		
2-2	1	1	"		
2-3	2	1	1:7	✓	
2-4	∅	1	"		mean = 1.4
TOTAL					

Figure 37. Case #2: Summary data on 14-month-old boy with sleep problems (Form 2 in Appendix). *Comments:* The clinician summarized data from the forms kept by the parents (see Figure 36 for a sample). This included the number of awakenings Malik had on his own, the number of scheduled awakenings, the ratio of milk to water in the bottle given in the night, and whether Malik was taken into the parents' bed in the night. We then calculated weekly means for Malik's self-awakenings.

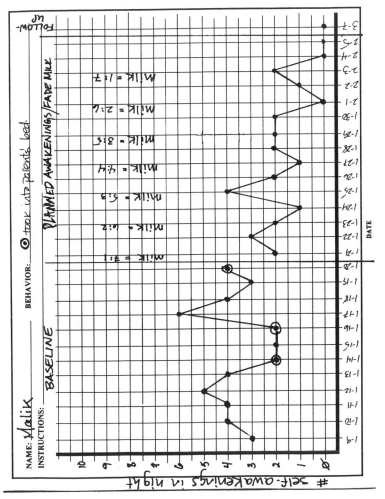

Figure 38. Case #2: Self-awakenings of 14-month-old boy with sleep problems. (Form 6 in Appendix.) *Comments:* This graph shows the number of Malik's self-awakenings before and after baseline. Days when the parents took him into their bed were circled and changes in milk–water ratio were noted.

came closer and closer to the time Malik had been put to be that evening. In this way, planned awakenings were eventually faded out.

Figure 37 is the clinician's summary of the information provided by the parents. Malik woke spontaneously a mean of 3.4 times in the first week of treatment and 3.8 times in the second week. By the end of the second week, the parents reported that Malik barely woke up during planned awakenings. As Figure 38 shows, by the end of the second week of treatment, Malik was no longer waking spontaneously.

Eventually, we told the parents they could discontinue collecting data, but that we would want them to measure for one more week in about a month. We then targeted sleep transition at bedtime, suggesting that his parents place Malik in his crib with his bottle of water at bedtime and pat him to sleep with his bottle of water. When he was going to sleep readily that way, we got them to gradually reduce the amount of time they would stay and pat him, letting him fall asleep on his own after a certain number of minutes of patting. We suggested they only come to the clinic every 2 weeks until this resulted in his going to sleep after only brief patting and comforting talk.

Follow Up

One month after the end of data collection, we asked the parents again to record for a week and bring in the data, which they did. As Figure 38 shows, Malik was not awakening and crying at all during the night.

CASE # 3: 3-YEAR-OLD GIRL WITH AGGRESSION AND NONCOMPLIANCE

Background Information

Mary was 3 years and 2 months of age and was brought to us by her parents because of physical aggression (especially biting) and noncompliance. She was an only child. The parents rated their marriage as "good." Both of them worked 40-hour weeks outside the home, with Mary going to daycare in a nearby neighbor's home during the day. That neighbor cared for four other children, and her threat to discontinue serving Mary because of her biting was what brought Mary's parents for help.

According to the parents, Mary had passed the developmental milestones normally and had no medical problems out of the ordinary. The Child Behavior Checklist (Achenbach, 1988) showed a clinically significant score for only the subscale "aggression." The Eyberg Child Behavior Inventory (Eyberg, 1974) showed a clinically significant Total Score of 126 (117 being sufficient for a clinically significant score) and a clinically significant Total Problem Score of 16 (11 being sufficient).

Measurement of and Intervention with Biting

Initial Data Collection on Biting

We decided to intervene first with biting, as that behavior threatened the other children's safety and Mary's continuation in daycare. We taught the mother how to use Form 8 to do ABC recording of Mary's biting at daycare and asked that she not only do a few minutes of such recording at daycare on 2 or more days during the coming week but, more important, that she train one of Mary's daycare workers in such recording. She agreed to spend at least 15 minutes doing the recording on at least 2 days and was confident that the daycare staff would be willing. The ABC recording is primarily for the purpose of discovering in what situations a particular behavior occurs and what consequences it produces. We were especially curious to see how the staff handled biting incidents. A sample of this recording may be seen in Figure 39.

Analysis and Plotting of ABC Data on Biting

The daycare staff reported to the mother that they had recorded every biting incident (see Figure 39). There were eight during the week. The mother reported that none occurred at home, as usual. According to the daycare data, all incidents occurred when Mary was with other children but when either no staff were in the room or when there was at least considerable distance between staff and her. Also, each incident appeared to be provoked by another child trying to take a toy that Mary was using. Staff handled each incident by reprimanding Mary and holding her on their lap for a few minutes of "cooling off."

We plotted the baseline as one data point for the week (see Figure 40) because the frequency per day would likely be only 0, 1, or 2.

Functional Formulation of Biting

Mary's biting was less frequent than either the parents or we had expected, from daycare reports, though certainly problematic. While such behavior could not be allowed to continue, it was obviously being reinforced by her retaining toys that she wanted to continue playing with. Another likely reinforcer was the extra attention (including the holding) she received from staff after her biting behavior. Finally, the reaction of the peer to being bitten may very well have been reinforcing.

NAME: Mary   BEHAVIOR(S): Biting

INSTRUCTIONS: BEFORE = Who was present, where the behavior occurred, & what was happening at the time?

BEHAVIOR = Describe the behavior exactly.

AFTER = Record who did what and how the child responded.

DATE	TIME	BEFORE (A)			BEHAVIOR(B)	AFTER (C)		
		Who?	Where?	What?		Who?	What?	Child's response
6-1	7:45	Peer (Sarah)	Daycare	Free Play — Sarah took a toy from M.	M. bit S. on arm + took back toy	Ms J.	Told M. "We don't bite." Time-out on Ms J's lap	M. cried for about 30 sec, then hugged teacher, went to Time-out
	10:15	Peer (James)	Daycare	Playing at "house" Center. James was "sweeping". M. cook's; T. asked to sweep	M. showed "No" bit J. on shoulder	S.	cried
						Mr. L.	Said "No biting. Tell J. you're sorry."	M. cried, refused to say "I'm sorry". M. L. held her on lap for Time-out, Told to 3
6-2	9:10	Peer (Emmy)	Daycare	Playing at "Cars" Center. E. playing quietly. E. grabbed toy, E. head onto toy	M. bit E. on hand	I	cried	
						E	Cried, let go of toy.	M. played E. toy briefly
						Mr. L.	Said "No biting. Sat on lap into	M. cried when Mr. L. Mr. L explained why it was important not to bite

Figure 39. Case #3: ABC recording of biting in daycare by 3-year-old girl with aggression and noncompliance. (Form 8 in Appendix.) *Comments:* The parent and daycare worker were asked to record times when Mary bit in daycare and the antecedents and consequences to them. They were encouraged to list the peer who was bitten and his or her response to the biting, as well as the response of the adult present.

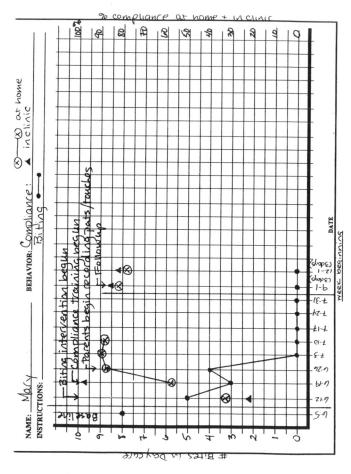

Figure 40. Case #3: Biting in 3-year-old girl at daycare and compliance at home and in clinic. (Form 6 in Appendix.) *Comments:* Baseline was taken in week one for biting and in week two for compliance at home and in clinic. Parents took data on compliance for the first and last 15 minutes of the day. After 3 weeks of over 80% compliance at home and after 5 weeks of no biting in daycare, the parents stopped taking data. Clinic probes were taken periodically and at follow up 2 and 5 months later.

Upon further discussion with daycare staff, it appeared that Mary tended to play with certain toys for long periods of time or even involve several different toys in the same play, leaving other children with little opportunity to use these toys. She ignored the other children's requests to use them, and on occasion would bite a child for merely asking. Thus we hypothesized that not only were there certain reinforcers for biting but also Mary, as an only child, had not been taught the need to share toys and how to do it.

Intervention with Biting

One of us went to the daycare home and helped the staff develop a way to teach Mary to share. Staff also agreed both to praise Mary throughout the day for "playing nicely" and to stop often and play with her when she was playing appropriately (and not soon after a biting incident) or to comment positively on what she was playing or making. We encouraged them to monitor how long Mary kept possession of any particular plaything and, if too long, to prompt her to let others use it. At the same time, we urged them to intervene if another child tried to take a toy from Mary, removing the toy from *both Mary's and the other child's* use for at least 15 minutes.

We introduced a star chart (Form 32, Appendix) on which staff were to stamp a "happy face" for each "activity" (period) of the day that Mary kept her mouth to herself. Staff were to start at the left and when one of the special squares was reached Mary was to be given a special sticker to put on the chart. Each day she took the day's star chart home to show her parents, who were to give lavish praise and hugs for Mary's earning lots of happy faces. Finally, if Mary did bite, we asked the staff to give her a 3-minute time out alone in a chair, and we taught them how to do this.

Continued Data Collection on Biting

Daycare staff continued to record biting, but they switched from the ABC recording to using the back of the star chart, which was a monthly calendar (Form 12). They simply made tally marks for each incident of biting.

Treatment Results with Biting

Figure 40 summarizes the main results of intervention for biting as well as other behaviors to be discussed below. We plotted the number of biting incidents per week (not per day as we often do), because biting frequency was low.

Mary's biting in daycare declined in frequency immediately and dropped to zero by the fourth week of treatment. Both daycare staff and Mary's parents were quite satisfied with these results.

Measurement of and Intervention with Noncompliance ──────────

Data Collection

Because the parents rarely saw biting at home, but were concerned about compliance, at the second session we taught them both how to tally instances of compliance and noncompliance, using Form 25 (see Figure 41). We saw little value in asking daycare staff to record compliance/noncompliance, because they were fairly satisfied with Mary's compliance; it was the biting that they could not tolerate. The parents identified bedtime and getting ready in the morning as the most difficult times, so compliance data were to be collected only at those two times, each for 15 minutes (using a kitchen timer to remind them when to stop).

We also evaluated compliance in the clinic, using a 20-minute contrived situation like that used by Forehand and McMahon (1981).

Analysis and Plotting of Data on Compliance

The parents' data from home (Figure 41 right had ordinate) showed that Mary complied with a mean of 28% of parental requests and commands in the morning and 26% at bedtime. We plotted these data as one data point, as the percent of requests complied with (Figure 40).

The compliance check in the clinic showed a frequency similar to that found by the parents. Mary complied with 23% of the mother's and father's requests and commands. During the clinic observation, we also noted that Mary interrupted her father frequently and the father had few positive interactions with Mary. The father's response to noncompliance was to repeat his request; if Mary persisted in not complying, he eventually either carried out the request himself or simply gave up asking her. The mother's handling of noncompliance was more emotional, generally, and more persistent. Sometimes she would take Mary by the hand and virtually guide her through complying, other times she would raise her voice, and once she swatted Mary on the bottom lightly for noncomplying. We repeated the clinic compliance check when we began teaching the parents how to develop compliance and on two later visits.

Functional Formulation of Noncompliance

As with most noncompliance, where a major source of reinforcement is simply the freedom to continue doing whatever one is already doing, we found this to be the case with Mary. When requesting something of Mary, both of her parents usually responded to being ignored or told "I don't want to" by letting her continue doing whatever she was doing, at least for a short time. For example, if she were told to get her pajamas on for bed, she could delay having to interrupt her ongoing

Mary:
OUR WEEK
(6-5 to 6-11)

Record #complies/noncomplies for 1st and last 15 min. of day.

	Monday	Tuesday	Wednesday	Thursday	Friday	Saturday	Sunday
A.M.	6 12	6-13	6-14	6-15	6-16	6-17	6-18
Complies	|||	||	||||			||	||||	||
noncomplies	ʜʜ̅ ||	ʜʜ̅ ||	||||	ʜʜ̅ ||||	ʜʜ̅ ||	ʜʜ̅ ||	ʜʜ̅ ||
P.M.							
Complies	||̸			|||	||	||	|||	0
noncomplies	|||	ʜʜ̅	ʜʜ̅	ʜʜ̅ ||	||||	||	ʜʜ̅ ||||
TOTAL FOR DAY	5/10	3/12	7/9	3/16	4/11	7/9	2/16
% compliance	50%	25%	78%	19%	36%	78%	12%

Comply = initiates a response within 5 sec. of a command.
noncomply = does not initiate a response

Figure 41. Case #3: Data compliance in 3-year-old girl with aggression and noncompliance. (Form 25 in Appendix.) *Comments:* After 1 week of baseline using the ABC form, Mary's parents were asked to keep track of compliance and noncompliance during only the first and last 15 minutes of Mary's day. Percent compliance daily and for the week were calculated by the therapist.

activity for several minutes by either ignoring them, actively refusing, or making up some reason why she could not do that just yet.

Also, noncompliance produced far more parental attention—in the form of persuasion, help in cleaning up, and so on—than did compliance, and the parents' occasional attempts at punishing noncompliance were too inconsistent and weak. In addition, the rewards for compliance seemed to be few, especially in comparison to the rewards of simply continuing her ongoing activity.

Intervention #1 with Noncompliance

After 1 week of daycare's treatment of Mary's biting, we began also treating her noncompliance at home. We taught both parents to praise, pat, hug, and otherwise show approval and affection to Mary frequently at times when she was following directions and otherwise cooperating. Further, we taught them how to use a calm "chair time out" for noncompliance (see Hembree-Kigin & McNeil, 1995)

Continued Data Collection on Noncompliance

We asked the parents to continue collecting data on compliance/noncompliance for two 15-minute periods each day (Figure 41).

Results of Intervention #1

Mary's compliance improved to better than 50% over the week (see Figure 40, noting percents in right ordinate). However, this is not an acceptable level. The parents reported that although they really wanted to increase their positives to Mary, they had difficulty remembering to do it, especially in the evening when they were tired. This is typical with parents, since compliance is not a very noticeable event, unlike noncompliance.

Intervention #2

To help the parents remember to praise, pat, hug, and so on, we taught them each to record their own positives and also record each others' (see Figure 42). They were to do this for only 30 minutes of each evening and only for 1 week if they succeeded in increasing the frequency of such positive feedback, so the task was not too onerous. The reason for their recording both themselves and the other person was to maximize the cuing and feedback for carrying through with the positives and for recording accurately.

Continued Data Collection

The parents were not only to record their positives to Mary but also to continue collecting data on Mary's compliance/noncompliance, using tally marks

NAME: Mary_____ MONTH: June_____ OBSERVER: _____
BEHAVIOR(S): 30 mins observation in evening; # pats/touches
INSTRUCTIONS: Each parent records own + other parent's positives

DATE	Mom watching news		Dad getting dinner		COMMENTS
	Mom's tally	Dad's tally	Mom's tally	Dad's tally	
6-19	III	II	I	I	
6-20	IIII	III I	III	II	
6-21	II	III	III	IIII	
6-22	IHT	IHT	III	II	
6-23	III	III	IIII	III	
6-24	I	II	IHT	IHT	
6-25	IIII	III	III	IIII	
TOTAL					

Figure 42. Case #3: Parent's data on positive interactions with 3-year-old girl with aggression and noncompliance. (Form 2 in Appendix.) *Comments:* Parents selected 30 minutes that were difficult times to remember to deliver positives. During that time, each parent observed both his or her own and the other parent's behavior, making tally marks for praise, pats, and other touches given to the child. This was recorded on pieces of tape on the parent's wrists and then placed on this recording sheet.

made on a small strip of clear tape that they put on their wrists. They later stuck those tapes on the data form shown in Figure 42.

Results of Intervention #2

Mary's compliance increased to 89% in the evening and, during our clinic check, to 93%. This was maintained for 3 weeks, at which time we continued to monitor biting at daycare and do spot checks in clinic for compliance. The parents no longer took data on compliance at home. After 5 weeks of no biting in daycare and parent satisfaction with compliance at home, we terminated treatment, asking that the parents participate in at least one follow-up, to be conducted in a month.

Follow Up

A month after reaching satisfactory behavior change, we phoned the parents, asked them again to record compliance/noncompliance data for 3 days, and to bring Mary in for a follow-up visit. We also asked that they get daycare staff to send home a record of any biting. The daycare data showed biting still to be at zero frequency, while the home data on compliance showed that behavior still to be at acceptable level (see Figure 40). We also conducted a check on Mary's compliance in the clinic during that visit and found it to be acceptable, though not quite as good as a month earlier.

We were somewhat concerned that Mary's compliance behavior would continue to decline, so we impressed upon the parents the importance of at least one further check in 3 more months, again obtaining 3 days' data before that return. They agreed and followed through. Again the compliance data from home and from our clinic probe showed a slight decline, but the biting data were still at zero. The parents were quite satisfied with these results, so we did not press for a further follow-up but instead encouraged them to come back if they had any further difficulties.

CASE # 4: 13-YEAR-OLD GIRL WITH RECURRENT ABDOMINAL PAIN

Background Information

Sarah was referred to us by her pediatrician and brought in by her mother. She was 13 and was reported to have frequent abdominal pain, resulting in her missing a great deal of school.

Sarah was the second of three children. Her parents divorced 3 years earlier, and all the children live with the mother. The mother's report indicated normal developmental milestones. Sarah had an early history of otitis media and of frequent colds. She had not begun menstruating.

Sarah complained of stomach pains several times each week. On one occasion her mother even took her to the emergency room due to acute pain, but no organic cause was found. Subsequent, thorough medical examinations had ruled out organic cause of her pains. Although she had a history of chronic constipation, current x-rays showed no residual stool.

The Child Behavior Checklist (Achenbach, 1992) showed elevated scores on "somatic complaints" and "depression" subscores. The Child Depression Inventory (Reynolds, Anderson, & Bartell, 1985) score was not in the clinical range.

Sarah's early colds and earaches often resulted in her missing school. She was currently missing an average of 2 days a week due to the abdominal pains. She was failing three subjects, although she was described as an average student prior to the current academic year.

Continuous Measurement

Data Collection

We asked Sarah to rate her pain at four specific times each day—using the Weekly Pain Record's 10-point scale (Form 26)—where ratings range from 0 = "no pain" to 10 = "extremely painful, I can't do anything when I have such pain" (see Figure 43). Her ratings were to be made by placing a data point on the graph above the hour when the rating is made, so that each day's record produces a small graph across the day. The connected dots give a graph of her pain across the day. This could help us functionally analyze environmental causes of the pain behavior.

The Weekly Pain Record also asks the person to indicate daily whether he or she took any medication, missed school or part of school, missed other activities, and had a bowel movement that day (and what size). The information on bowel movements was included because sometimes recurrent abdominal pain is related to constipation, a problem fairly easily remedied. Sarah preferred to be the only person taking the data, although her mother was quite willing to record all but the pain rating.

Data Plotting and Analysis

Although the Pain Record showed a small graph for each day, we also wanted graphs that would show overall progress, so we graphed the mean pain rating for the week, the amount of school missed each week, and the mean number of bowel movements (see Figure 44).

The week's data on pain (Figure 43) showed a very consistent phenomenon: on school days Sarah experienced the most pain in the morning, and it eased steadily through the day, with generally mild pain in the evening. We also saw that

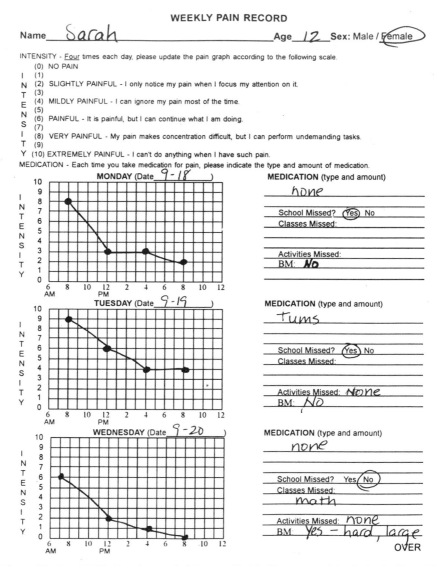

Figure 43. Case #4: Weekly pain record of 13-year-old girl with recurrent abdominal pain. (Form 26, Appendix.) *Comments:* Sarah kept a record of abdominal pain at four set times per day. She also kept information on medication, activities missed, and bowel movements and kept track of the antecedents and consequences to the pain at each of the four times. A single sample is included here. (Thanks to Dr. Keith Allen for sharing this form with us.)

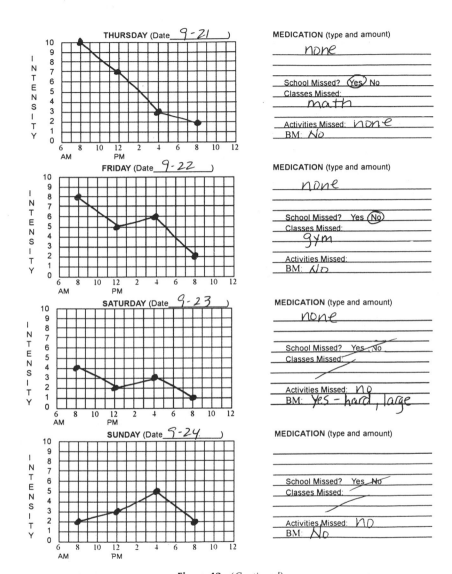

THURSDAY (Date 9-21)

MEDICATION (type and amount)

School Missed? (Yes) No
Classes Missed:
math
Activities Missed: none
BM: No

FRIDAY (Date 9-22)

MEDICATION (type and amount)

School Missed? Yes (No)
Classes Missed:
gym
Activities Missed:
BM: No

SATURDAY (Date 9-23)

MEDICATION (type and amount)

School Missed? Yes No
Classes Missed:

Activities Missed: no
BM: Yes - hard, large

SUNDAY (Date 9-24)

MEDICATION (type and amount)

School Missed? Yes No
Classes Missed:

Activities Missed: no
BM: No

Figure 43. (*Continued*)

Please put a check mark in front of each thing that happened before the pain occurred,
and each thing that happened after the pain occurred.

What Happened Before Pain?

☐ Ate something _Did not eat – felt_
Specify what _____ sick. _____
_____

☐ Drank something _____
Specify what _____
_____

☐ Glare or bright light
☐ Weather or temperature change
☐ Too much sleep
☐ Strong odors, fumes
☐ Game of competition
☒ Worried about something
☐ Sad/unhappy
☒ Difficult school work or test
☐ Angry about something
☐ Problem/fight with parents
☐ Problem/fight with friends
☐ Concentrated hard on something
☐ Something embarrassing happened
☐ Too much physical activity
☒ Woke up in morning with pain
☐ Woke up in night with pain
☐ Hunger
☐ I have my menstrual period (Day of period:_____)
☐ Other (please specify) _____
_____

_9/18 – 8:00 a.m._

What Happened During/After Pain?

☐ Took medication (indicate type and how much) ___

☒ Missed school
☐ Missed one or more classes
Specify which class(es) _____
_____

☐ Did not complete homework
☐ Could not get out of bed in morning
☐ Chose a quiet activity to manage the pain
☒ Did not complete chores
Specify which chores missed _make bed,_
feed dog
☐ Missed practice/appointment/lesson.
Specify which practice/appointment(s) ___
_____

☐ Asked parent for help
☐ Asked parent for medication
☐ Tried to ignore pain
☐ Slept
☒ Rested
☐ Turned off lights, shut blinds, shades, or shutters
☐ Turned off sounds (T.V., music)
☐ Ate or drank something
☐ Applied heat/cold to pain location
☒ Massaged pain location
☐ Got a massage from someone else
☐ Started exercise or other recreation
☐ Cried
☐ Tried to distract self (listen to music, watch TV)
☐ Practiced relaxation
☐ Tried to remain active
☐ Did normal activity/routine
☒ Talked to parent/friend about pain
☐ Had a bowel movement
☐ Other (please specify) : _Watched T.V._
at Grandma's

Figure 43. (*Continued*)

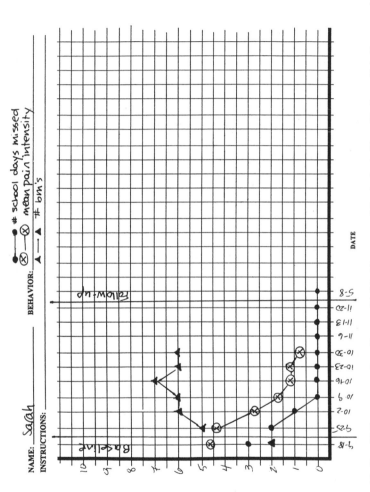

Figure 44. Case #4: Summary graph on 13-year-old girl with recurrent abdominal pain (Form 6 in Appendix). *Comments:* Note that after intervention, Sarah's pain ratings decreased, as did school absences. This coincided with more regular bowel habits. This was maintained at 6 months' follow-up.

Sarah had bowel movements infrequently, and when she had them they were hard and large. She missed 3 days of school (all due to abdominal pain), and when she went to school, the class she missed most often in this 1 week baseline was math. Medication (at least Tums) had no apparent effect on her pain.

In discussing the week with the mother, we learned that Sarah's complaints began immediately upon arising in the morning and that she missed breakfast on 4 days due to these complaints. On the days when she missed school, she stayed with her maternal grandmother, who is ailing and spends most of the day on the couch watching TV. Sarah joins her in this when she is there.

Functional Case Formulation

It appeared that Sarah's abdominal pain was initially due to two things: (a) infrequent bowel movements (although she did not show residual stool on x-rays, she showed signs of constipation); and (b) her having fallen behind in school (partly due to a bout with the flu), making schoolwork especially aversive for her. Subsequently, her pain behaviors were probably being reinforced by avoiding school (perhaps especially math) and by staying home with her grandmother where she could watch TV.

Intervention and Results

Treatment

Our intervention addressed several things at once. First, we addressed the constipation by developing, in collaboration with her pediatrician, a dietary regimen involving high-fiber foods, ample fluids, and reduced milk products.

Second, we addressed the school achievement problem by helping the mother arrange tutoring for Sarah. The school psychologist helped identify a neighboring college student who was happy to help for a small hourly wage. Also, Sarah's math teacher volunteered to help Sarah on Tuesdays right after school.

Third, we addressed the school attendance problem by convincing the mother that—although Sarah was experiencing real pain—the pain behaviors were still being reinforced by avoiding school, by watching TV with the grandmother, and possibly by sympathetic attention. We were not able to convince the grandmother of this, but we did persuade the mother to arrange for Sarah to stay with an aunt and uncle if she truly had to stay home from school because of verified illness (e.g., a temperature of at least 100), but not for abdominal pain. The mother said that the aunt would see that Sarah's day was spent in bed or doing schoolwork and that it did not include watching TV or other entertaining activities.

Finally, we explained to Sarah how stress can lead to abdominal pain and we offered to conduct relaxation training. She agreed to try it, and after the first session she agreed to proceed with it.

Continued Data Collection

Sarah continued to complete the Weekly Pain Record, including the record of bowel movements. In addition, her mother kept a daily record of Sarah's diet, so that we could be sure it was of a type that should help with her constipation.

After the ninth week of seeing Sarah, we dropped all measurement except the school attendance, which was continued for 4 further weeks, during which we saw Sarah and the mother only every 2 weeks.

Treatment Results

As Figure 44 shows, Sarah's bowel movements became much more regular by the second week of her new diet (5 out of 7 days per week, with soft-formed consistency). With some initial complaint, she attended school 3 days the first week, 4 days the next week, and then every day for the subsequent 7 weeks. Finally, Sarah's pain ratings gradually declined. The mother was quite satisfied, although Sarah was still concerned that she continued to experience some pain (mean = .8 on the last week). By the seventh week, we asked Sarah to record only whether she was attending school, as shown in Figure 45. In spite of occasional reports of pain (noted anecdotally on the form), it was not interfering with her every-

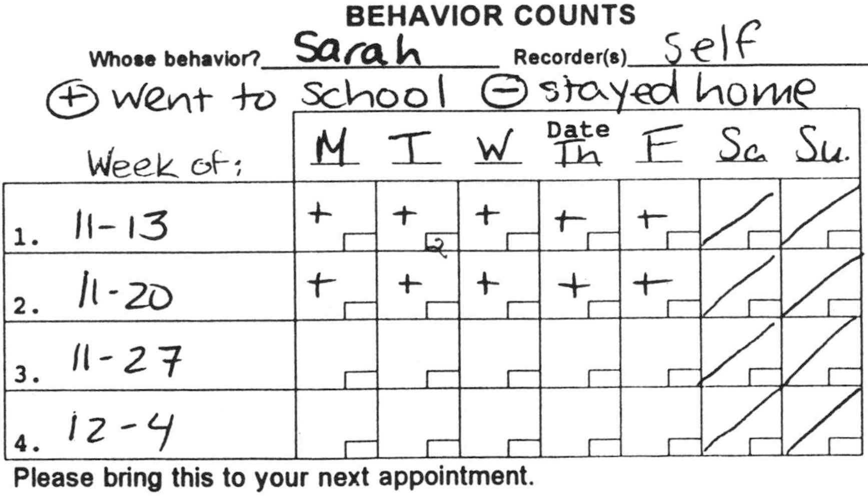

BEHAVIOR COUNTS

Whose behavior? Sarah Recorder(s) Self

(+) went to school (−) stayed home

Week of:	M	T	W	Date Th	F	Sa.	Su.
1. 11-13	+	+ 2	+	+	+	/	/
2. 11-20	+	+	+	+	+	/	/
3. 11-27						/	/
4. 12-4						/	/

Please bring this to your next appointment.

Figure 45. Case #4: Record of school attendence by 13-year-old girl with recurrent abdominal pain (Form 10 in Appendix). *Comments:* After 6 weeks of keeping daily pain records, Sarah was asked simply to keep a record of whether or not she missed school and to note in the small box any days she experienced pain above a rating of "1."

day life and she was attending school. Consequently we ended treatment, urging her to contact us if the problem returned in any form.

Follow Up

Sarah's mother reported by phone that Sarah had missed 5 or 6 days of school since they had been in to see us and that on only 2 or 3 of those days was it due to Sarah's abdominal pain. We urged the mother to stick with her plan to never keep Sarah home for abdominal pain.

Sarah agreed that if we would mail her a blank Weekly Pain Record, she would complete it again for 1 week and mail it back to us. Neither she nor her mother wished to come to the clinic, however, and Sarah did not wish to report on her bowel movements. She sounded much more confident over the phone than she had 6 months earlier.

Sarah's ratings showed only 1 day when her pain was above a zero, and that was at only one of the four times. She was not absent from school or any part of it during the week.

References

Achenbach, T. M. (1988). *Manual for the Child Behavior Checklist/2–3.* Burlington, VT: University of Vermont, Department of Psychiatry.

Achenbach, T. M. (1991). *Manual for the Child Behavior Checklist/4–18 and 1992 profile.* Burlington, VT: University of Vermont, Department of Psychiatry.

Allen, K. D., & Mathews, J. R. (1998). Behavior management of recurrent pain in children. In T.S. Watson & F. Gresham (Eds.), *Child behavior therapy: Ecological considerations in assessment, treatment, and evaluation* (pp. 263–285). New York: Plenum.

Alessi, G. (1988). Direct observation methods for emotional/behavior problems. In E. S. Shapiro & T. R. Kratochwill (Eds.), *Behavioral assessment in schools.* New York: Guilford.

Association for Advancement of Behavior Therapy. (1991). *What to expect from psychotherapy.* [Brochure] Washington, DC: Author.

Baer, D. M. (1981) *How to plan for generalization.* Lawrence, KS: H & H Enterprises.

Baer, D. M., & Fowler, S. (1984). How should we measure the potential of self-control procedures for generalized educational outcomes? In W. L Heward, T. E. Heron, D. S. Hill, & J. Trap-Porter (Eds.), *Focus on behavior analysis in education* (pp. 145–161). Columbus, OH: Charles E. Merrill.

Barkley, R. A. (1987). *Defiant children: Parent–teacher assignments.* New York: Guilford.

Barkley, R. A. (1990). *Attention deficit hyperactivity disorder.* New York: Guilford.

Barlow, D. H. (1980). Behavior therapy: The next decade. *Behavior Therapy, 11,* 315–328.

Barlow, D. H., Hayes, S. C., & Nelson, R. O. (1984). *The scientist-practitioner: Research and accountability in clinical and educational settings.* New York: Pergamon Press.

Browning, C. H., & Browning, B. J. (1996). *How to partner with managed care: A "do-it-yourself kit" for building working relationships and getting steady referrals* (expanded edition). New York: John Wiley & Sons.

Carter, R. K. (1983). *The accountable agency.* Beverly Hills, CA: Sage.

Chamberlain, P., & Reid, J. R. (1987). Parent observation and report of child symptoms. *Behavioral Assessment, 10,* 97–109.

Cone, J. D., & Hawkins, R. P. (1977). Introduction. In J. D. Cone & R. P. Hawkins (Eds.), *Behavioral assessment: New directions in clinical psychology* (pp. xiii–xxiv). New York: Brunner/Mazel.

Cormier, W. H., & Cormier, L. S. (1979). *Interviewing strategies for helpers: Fundamental skills and cognitive behavioral interventions* (3rd ed.). Pacific Grove, CA: Brooks/Cole.

DiGiuseppe, R., Linscott, J., & Jilton, R. (1996). Developing the therapeutic alliance in child-adolescent psychotherapy. *Applied & Preventive Psychology, 5,* 85–100.

Dornelas, E. A., Correll, R. E., Lothstein, L., Wilber, C., & Goethe, J. W. (1996). Designing and implementing outcome evaluations: Some guidelines for practitioners. *Psychotherapy, 33,* 237–245.

Edmunds, M., Frank, R., Hogan, M., McCarty, D., Robinson-Beale, R., & Weisner, C. (1997). *Managing managed care: Quality improvement in behavioral health.* Washington, DC: National Academy Press.

Ersner-Hershfield, S. M., Connors, G. J., & Maisto, S. A. (1981). Clinical and experimental utility of refundable deposits. *Behaviour Research and Therapy, 19,* 455–457.

Evans, I. M., & Meyer, L. H. (1985). *An educative approach to behavior problems: A practical decision model for interventions with severely handicapped learners.* Baltimore, MD: Paul H. Brookes.\

Eyberg, S. M. (1974). *Eyberg Child Behavior Inventory.* (Available from Sheila Eyberg, Department of Clinical and Health Psychology, Box 100165 HSC, University of Florida, Gainesville, FL 32610).

Fabry, B. D., Hawkins, R. P., & Luster, W. C. (1994). Monitoring outcomes of services to children and youths with severe emotional disorders: An economical follow-up procedure for mental health and child care agencies. *The Journal of Mental Health Administration, 21,* 271–281.

Forehand, R. L., & McMahon, R. J. (1981). *Helping the noncompliant child: A clinician's guide to parent training.* New York: Guilford.

Hartmann, D. P. (Ed.) (1982). *New directions for methodology of behavior science: Using observers to study behavior.* San Francisco: Jossey-Bass.

Hawkins, R. P. (1979). The functions of assessment: Implications for selection and development of devices for assessing repertoires in clinical, educational, and other settings. *Journal of Applied Behavior Analysis, 12,* 501–516.

Hawkins, R. P. (1986). Selection of target behaviors. In R. O. Nelson & S. C. Hayes (Eds.), *Conceptual foundations of behavioral assessment* (pp. 331–385). New York: Guilford.

Hawkins, R. P. (1989). Developing potent behavior-change technologies: An invitation to cognitive behavior therapists. *The Behavior Therapist, 12,* 126–131.

Hawkins, R. P. (1991). Is social validity what we are interested in? Argument for a functional approach. *Journal of Applied Behavior Analysis, 24,* 205–213.

Hawkins, R. P., & Dobes, R. W. (1977). Behavioral definitions in applied behavior analysis: Explicit or implicit. In B. C. Etzel, J. M. LeBlanc, & D. M. Baer (Eds.), *New developments in behavioral research: Theory, methods, and applications* (pp. 167–188). Hillsdale, NJ: Lawrence Erlbaum Associates.

Hawkins, R. P., & Hursh, D. E. (1992). Levels of research for clinical practice: It isn't as hard as you think. *The West Virginia Journal of Psychological Research and Practice, 1,* 61–71.

Hembree-Kigin, T. L., & McNeil, C. B. (1995). *Parent-child interaction therapy.* New York: Plenum.

Johnson, L. D., & Shaha, S. (1996). Improving quality in psychotherapy. *Psychotherapy, 33,* 225–235.

Kanter, F. H., Cox, L. E., Greiner, J.M., & Karoly, P. (1974). Contracts, demand characteristics, and self-control. *Journal of Personality and Social Psychology, 30,* 605–619.

Kelley, M. L. (1990). *School-home notes: Promoting children's classroom success.* New York: Guilford.

Levy, R. L. (1977). Relationship of an overt commitment to task compliance in behavior therapy. *Journal of Behavior Therapy and Experimental Psychiatry, 8,* 25–29.

Martin, G., & Pear, J. (1996). *Behavior modification: What it is and how to do it* (5th ed.). Upper Saddle River, NJ: Prentice-Hall.

McFall, R. M. (1977). Analogue methods in behavioral assessment: Issues and prospects. In J. D. Cone & R. P. Hawkins (Eds.), *Behavioral assessment: New directions in clinical psychology* (pp. 152–177). New York: Brunner/Mazel.

Meyer, L., & Janney, R. (1989). User-friendly measures of meaningful outcomes: Evaluating behavioral interventions. *Journal of the Association for Persons with Severe Handicaps, 14,* 263–270.

Ogles, B. M., Lambert, M. J., & Masters, K. S. (1996). *Assessing outcome in clinical practice.* Boston: Allyn and Bacon.

O'Neill, R. E., Horner, R. H., Albin, R. W., Storey, K, & Sprague, J. R. (1990). *Functional analysis of problem behavior: A practical assessment guide.* Sycamore, IL: Sycamore Publishing Company.

Patterson, G. R., Reid, J. B., Jones, R. R., & Conger, R. (1975). *A social learning approach to family intervention, Vol. 1: Families with aggressive children.* Eugene, OR: Castalia.

Reynolds, W.M., Anderson, G., & Bartell, N. (1985). Measuring depression in children: A multimethod assessment investigation. *Journal of Abnormal Child Psychology, 13,* 513–526.

Shelton, J. L., & Levy, R. L. (1981). *Behavioral assignments and treatment compliance.* Champaign, IL: Research Press.

Sperry, L., Brill, P. L, Howard, K. I., & Grissom, G. R. (1996). *Treatment outcomes in psychotherapy and psychiatric interventions.* New York: Brunner/Mazel.

Stokes, T. F., & Baer, D.M. (1977). An implicit technology of generalization. *Journal of Applied Behavior Analysis, 10,* 349–367.

Touchette, P. E., MacDonald, R. F., & Langer, S. N. (1985). A scatter plot for identifying stimulus control of problem behavior. *Journal of Applied Behavior Analysis, 18,* 343–351.

Wolf, M. M. (1978). Social validity: The case for subjective measurement, or how behavior analysis is finding its heart. *Journal of Applied Behavior Analysis, 11,* 203–214.

Wright, J. H., & Davis, D. (1994). The therapeutic relationship in cognitive-behavioral therapy: Patient perceptions and therapist responses. *Cognitive and Behavioral Practice, 1,* 25–45.

Appendix

The reader is welcome to copy any of these forms. Adaptation to individual needs is also encouraged

NAME: _____ MONTH:_____ OBSERVER: _____
BEHAVIOR(S):_____
INSTRUCTIONS:_____

DATE		COMMENTS
TOTAL		

Form 1. Generic Vertical Form. *Comments:* This can be adapted for any type of recording. Adding columns by hand can allow the clinician to tailor the form to any behavior.

NAME: _____ MONTH: _____ OBSERVER: _____

BEHAVIOR(S): _____

DATE					COMMENTS
TOTAL					

Form 2. Adaptation of Form 1. *Comments:* For four behaviors or intervals.

NAME: _____ MONTH:_____ OBSERVER: _____

BEHAVIOR(S):_____

DAY		COMMENTS
1		
2		
3		
4		
5		
6		
7		
8		
9		
10		
11		
12		
13		
14		
15		
16		
17		
18		
19		
20		
21		
22		
23		
24		
25		
26		
27		
28		
29		
30		
31		
TOTAL		

Form 3. Adaptation of Form 1. *Comments:* For monthly recording. Adding columns can allow the clinician to record more than one behavior. We often use this for encopresis, recording number of soilings, number of bowel movements in toilet, high-fiber foods eaten, medication/suppositories used, amount of exercise, and number of glasses of water.

NAME: _____ MONTH: _____ OBSERVER: _____

BEHAVIOR(S): _____

DATE		COMMENTS
TOTAL		

Form 4. Generic Horizontal Form. *Comments:* Can be adapted for almost any type of recording. Make as many columns as needed.

NAME: _____ MONTH: _____ OBSERVER: _____

BEHAVIOR(S): _____

DATE																				COMMENTS
TOTAL																				

Form 5. Adaptation of Form 4. *Comments*: Twelve behaviors, samples, or intervals.

NAME: _____ BEHAVIOR: _____

INSTRUCTIONS: _____

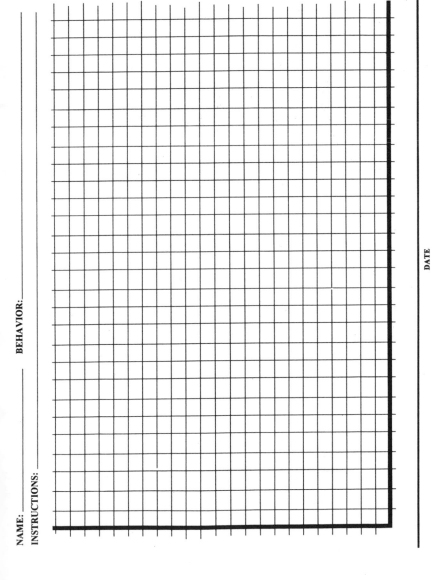

DATE

Form 6. Graph. *Comments:* Put dates along the X-axis and the type of measurement (e.g., frequency, duration) and behavior along the Y-axis. Note any important events or changes of intervention on the graph with an arrow pointing to the datum.

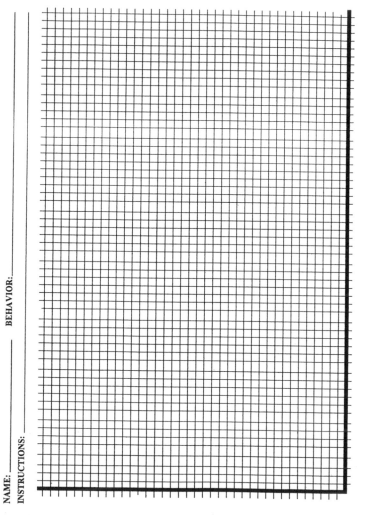

NAME: _____

INSTRUCTIONS: _____

BEHAVIOR: _____

DATE

Form 7. Graph.

ABC RECORDING FORMS

NAME: _____   BEHAVIOR(S): _____

INSTRUCTIONS : BEFORE = Who was present, where the behavior occurred, & what was happening at the time?

BEHAVIOR = Describe the behavior exactly.

AFTER = Record who did what and how the child responded.

DATE	TIME	BEFORE (A)			BEHAVIOR(B)	AFTER (C)		
		Who?	Where?	What?		Who?	What?	Child's response

Form 8. Assessment of Antecedents, Behaviors, and Consequences (ABC): Open-Ended. *Comments:* This is open-ended, in comparison to Form 9. It allows the adult to make more comments but is more time-consuming than Form 9.

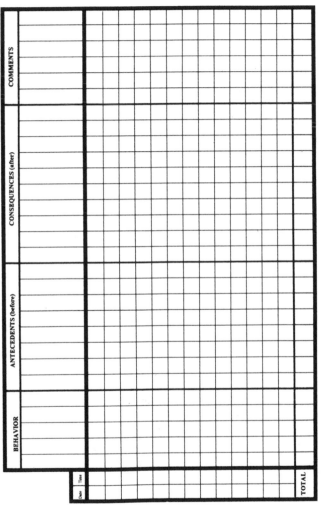

NAME: _____ BEHAVIOR(S): _____

INSTRUCTIONS 1. TOP COLUMNS: Fill in specific targeted BEHAVIORS, ANTECEDENTS (e.g., location, activity, persons present, type of instruction) and
CONSEQUENCES (e.g., positive rewards socials, negative consequences such as time-out reprimand) & COMMENTS (other specifics).

2. EACH TIME: THE TARGETED BEHAVIOR OCCURS, write in date & time; check all columns that apply.

	BEHAVIOR	ANTECEDENTS (before)	CONSEQUENCES (after)	COMMENTS

Date Time

TOTAL

Form 9. Assessment of Antecedents, Behaviors, and Consequences (ABC): Checklist. *Comments:* Based on the adult's observations, specifics can be written in and the parent can add others as they occur. This is less time-consuming but may not give as much detail as Form 8. This form is adapted from O'Neill et. al (1990), reprinted with permission from Wadsworth Publishing.

FREQUENCY RECORDING FORMS ———————————————————

Name: _____

Date:

Behaviors	__	__	__	__	__	__	__	__
1.								
2.								
3.								
4.								

Please bring this to your next appointment.

Form 10. Four Behaviors Weekly: Index Card. *Comments:* This card is versatile and can also be used to record four behaviors or situations or as a monthly data form. Clients report liking this compact form, which can be put on the refrigerator or placed in a pocket or purse.

NAME: _____ MONTH: _____ OBSERVER: _____

INSTRUCTIONS: _____

BEHAVIOR/SITUATION:	SUNDAY	MONDAY	TUESDAY	WED	THURS	FRIDAY	SAT	Total Week	Ave Week
WEEK 1: 1.									
2.									
___ to ___ 3.									
4.									
WEEK 2: 1.									
2.									
___ to ___ 3.									
4.									
WEEK 3: 1.									
2.									
___ to ___ 3.									
4.									
WEEK 4: 1.									
2.									
___ to ___ 3.									
4.									
WEEK 5: 1.									
2.									
___ to ___ 3.									
4.									

Form 11. Five Weeks, Four Behaviors or Situations. *Comments:* Although this gives a summary of an entire month at a glance, it may be cumbersome for a family to transport back and forth to sessions. Weekly data forms, such as Form 10, are usually more useful.

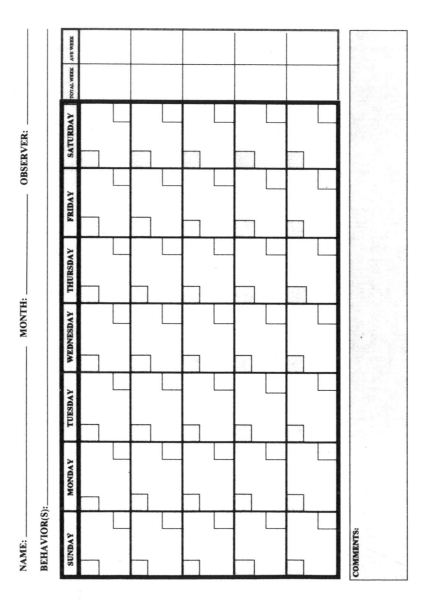

NAME: _____   MONTH: _____   OBSERVER: _____

BEHAVIOR(S): _____

SUNDAY	MONDAY	TUESDAY	WEDNESDAY	THURSDAY	FRIDAY	SATURDAY	TOTAL WEEK	AVE WEEK

COMMENTS: _____

Form 12. Monthly Calendar. *Comments:* Record day of the month in shaded upper left-hand square and summary data (e.g., total or mean) in the lower right-hand square.

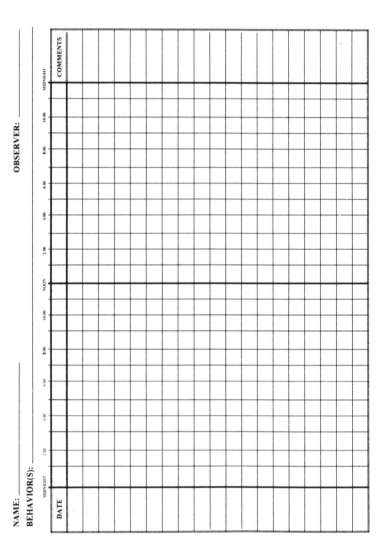

Form 13. Duration Recording. *Comments:* We often use this for a sleep record. The parent is asked to shade in the times when the child is awake or asleep and use an arrow to indicate times he or she gets in or out of bed. This form is adapted from Ferber, R. (1985), *Solve your child's sleep problems.* New York: Simon & Schuster.

INTERVAL/MOMENTARY TIME SAMPLING RECORDING

NAME: _____ DATE:_____ OBSERVER: _____
BEHAVIOR(S):_____

INSTRUCTIONS: Record "+" if behavior occurred in interval; draw a line through the interval if it did not occur.

Minute begins	1-10	11-20	21-30	31-40	41-50	51-60	Minute ends
0							1
1							2
2							3
3							4
4							5
5							6
6							7
7							8
8							9
9							10
10							11
11							12
12							13
13							14
14							15
15							16
16							17
17							18
18							19
19							20

TOTAL # INTERVALS: [   ]

% OF INTERVALS: [   ]

COMMENTS:

Form 14. Interval Recording (Clinic Observations). *Comments:* 20 minutes' interval recording in 10-second intervals. This is particularly useful in the clinic for direct observation of a behavior, such as a habit disorder or parents' attention to the child. It is not often useful if the data are to be recorded by a family member, because recording in consecutive 10-second intervals makes the task very intensive.

Child _____ Date _____ Coder _____
Adult: _____ Parent _____ Clinician

_____ (___-SECOND INTERVALS)

CONDITION:

INTERVAL	1	2	3	4	5	6	7	8	9	10	11	12	13	14	15	16	17	18	19	20	T

CONDITION:

INTERVAL	1	2	3	4	5	6	7	8	9	10	11	12	13	14	15	16	17	18	19	20	T

CONDITION:

INTERVAL	1	2	3	4	5	6	7	8	9	10	11	12	13	14	15	16	17	18	19	20	T

CONDITION:

INTERVAL	1	2	3	4	5	6	7	8	9	10	11	12	13	14	15	16	17	18	19	20	T

Form 15. Interval Recording (Clinic Observations). *Comments:* Label observation and interval length at top. Under "Condition," describe any particulars (e.g., "alone," "play," "high demand"). Under "Interval" list the behavior to be observed. Check its occurrence in each interval. "T" at the end stands for "Total" number of intervals the behavior was observed. This can be used for momentary time sampling as well.

NAME: _____ MEAL: B L D Snack

DATE: _____ TOTAL TIME: _____ TEXTURE: Pureed ____ Strained ____ Junior ____ Table ____

EATING BEHAVIORS

1-Minute Intervals		1	2	3	4	5	6	7	8	9	10	11	12	13	14	15	16	17	18	19	20
FRUIT:	Accept																				
1.	Self-Feed																				
2	Mouth Empty																				
3.	Refusal																				
4.	Expel																				
VEGETABLE:	Accept																				
1.	Self-Feed																				
2.	Mouth Empty																				
3.	Refusal																				
4.	Expel																				
BREAD:	Accept																				
1.	Self-Feed																				
2.	Mouth Empty																				
3.	Refusal																				
4.	Expel																				
MEAT:	Accept																				
1.	Self-Feed																				
2.	Mouth Empty																				
3.	Refusal																				
4.	Expel																				
LIQUID:	Accept																				
1.	Self-Feed																				
2.	Mouth Empty																				
3.	Refusal																				
4.	Expel																				
NEG. BHVR: 1.																					
2.																					
3.																					

(Left margin label: CHILD)

1-Minute Intervals		1	2	3	4	5	6	7	8	9	10	11	12	13	14	15	16	17	18	19	20
COAX																					
PROMPT TO EAT																					
POSITIVE/NEUTRAL	Social																				
	Tangible																				
NEGATIVE																					
OTHER 1.																					
2.																					
TIME-OUT: 1. Parent Turns																					
2. Removes Food/Toy																					
3. Turns Child																					

(Left margin label: PARENT)

Form 16. Eating Behaviors (Clinic Observations). *Comments:* List the foods under the food group. Mark frequency under each interval.

CHILD BEHAVIOR

SUMMARY	Volume Consumed	Accepts	Self-Feed	Mouth Empty	Refusal	Expels
Fruit						
Vegetable						
Bread						
Meat						
Liquid						
OVERALL TOTAL						

Total Negative Behavior   1. _____

(# intervals)   2. _____

                         3. _____

PARENT BEHAVIOR

	TOTAL	Child Behavior within 1 interval *		
		+ Accepts/ Self-Feeds	- Other	
Prompt				Antecedents
Coax				Antecedents
Positive				Consequences
Negative				Consequences
Time-Out				
Other				

* Record only child behaviors that occur within 1 interval of the parent's behavior.

Comments:

_____

_____

_____

_____

Instructions

List foods on tray; when recording bites, indicate numbers in interval (1-3) of food.
Intervals are of 1-minute duration.

Operational Definitions

Child

Accept	=	Takes bite offered by parent (record frequency)
Self-Feed	=	Takes bite by self, may or may not be parent initiated (record frequency)
Mouth Empty	=	Child swallows food in mouth (record frequency)
Refusal	=	Turns head, closes mouth, or pushes away food (record frequency)
Expel	=	Food is spit out (record frequency)

Negative Child Behavior: Any negative vocal, verbal or physical behavior (e.g., cry, scream, "no," "you're stupid," up from table, throw food, hit or kick adult). List specific behavior. Record as partial interval (check once if occurs anytime during the interval)

Parent

Prompt to eat: Parent instructs child to take a bite. Score only for first prompt for each bite.

Coax: Parent repeats prompt or plays games to try to get the child to eat (e.g., "Here comes the airplane" or "Look how good Jamey is eating"). Record frequency.

Parent Negative: Any negative comment or action such as a reprimand, physical coercion, or physical aggression. List specific behavior. Record frequency.

Time-Out:
1.	Parent turns	=	clear, discrete ignore
2.	Removes food/toy	=	tray is cleared momentarily
3.	Turns child	=	child's chair is turned away

Record as partial interval (check if occurs any time during the interval).

Form 16. (*Continued*)

REINFORCER ASSESSMENT

Place all potential reinforcers within easy access of the child. Before begining, demonstrate the use of each. For each 15-second interval, place a checkmark below the item the child contacts. Allow 5 minutes of free access. At bottom, record total number of intervals for each item, then rank them accordingly.

Potential Reinforcer:	Interval																			
	1	2	3	4	5	6	7	8	9	10	11	12	13	14	15	16	17	18	19	20
#1:																				
#2:																				
#3:																				
#4:																				
#5:																				
#6:																				
#7:																				
#8:																				
#9:																				
#10:																				
Total Intervals:																				

RANK ORDER TOP 5 POTENTIAL REINFORCERS:

1. _____

2. _____

3. _____

4. _____

5. _____

Form 17. Interval Recording: Reinforcer Assessment (Clinic Observations). *Comments:* Place several potential reinforcers within reach of the child and check all items contacted in each interval. This is most useful for very young or nonverbal children.

REINFORCER ASSESSMENT

NAME: _____ DATE _____ OBSERVER: _____

HOW OFTEN ARE YOU CHECKING? EVERY: _____ hour _____ minutes

TIME	WHERE?	What was s(he) doing?	Who chose the activity?	How enjoyable is it? (Rate 0-5)	
				Child	Adult

Form 18. Interval Recording: Reinforcer Assessment (Home Observations). *Comments:* Have parent note at regular intervals what the child is doing and rate the child's apparent or reported enjoyment. This then can be used along with a formal reinforcer assessment in clinic to determine potential reinforcers.

Name: _____   **Behavior:** _____

Instructions: _____

INTERVALS

Date:																								

Form 19. Interval Recording (Home Observations). *Comments:* Numbers can be variable (as in Figure 11) or fixed (as in Figure 12).

Client: _____ Behavior: _____ Month: _____

☐ _____ ◪ _____ ■ _____ ⊞ Not observed

Instructions: _____

_____

_____

Date	1	2	3	4	5	6	7	8	9	10	11	12	13	14	15	16	17	18	19	20	21	22	23	24	25	26	27	28	29	30	31
6:00																															
6:30																															
7:00																															
7:30																															
8:00																															
8:30																															
9:00																															
9:30																															
10:00																															
10:30																															
11:00																															
11:30																															
12:00																															
12:30																															
1:00																															
1:30																															
2:00																															
2:30																															
3:00																															
3:30																															
4:00																															
4:30																															
5:00																															
5:30																															
6:00																															
6:30																															
7:00																															
7:30																															
8:00																															
8:30																															
9:00																															
9:30																															
10:00																															
10:30																															
11:00																															
11:30																															
12:00																															
12:30																															
1:00																															
1:30																															
2:00																															
2:30																															
3:00																															
3:30																															
4:00																															
4:30																															
5:00																															
5:30																															

(A.M. covers 6:00–11:30; P.M. covers 12:00–11:30; A.M. covers 12:00–5:30)

Form 20. Scatterplot (Home Observations). *Comments:* On this form, the client is asked to use different marks for different frequencies (e.g., a blank box can indicate no occurrence, a diagonal slash indicates occasional occurrence, and a colored-in box indicate high frequency). A vertical line indicates no opportunity to observe. This is particularly useful for high frequency behaviors such as self-injurious behavior. This form is adapted from Touchette et al. (1985).

Target Behaviors For: _____   Date: _____

1. _____   3. _____
2. _____   4. _____

HR/DY	7	8	9	10	11	12	1	2	3	4	5	6	7	8	9	10	
S																	
M																	
T																	
W																	
T																	
F																	
S																	

Please bring this to your next appointment.

Form 21. Interval Recording Weekly: Index Card (Home Observations). *Comments:* Note that this can be used for up to four behaviors. Put the number in the appropriate box. Any given interval could have up to four numbers recorded.

NAME: _____ DATES:_____ OBSERVER: _____

BEHAVIOR(S):_____

	SUNDAY	MONDAY	TUESDAY	WEDNESDAY	THURSDAY	FRIDAY	SATURDAY
7-7:30 am							
7:30-8:00							
8:00-8:30							
8:30-9:00							
9:00-9:30							
9:30-10:00							
10:00-10:30							
10:30-11:00							
11:00-11:30							
11:30-12:00							
12-12:30pm							
12:30-1:00							
1:00-1:30							
1:30-2:00							
2:00-2:30							
2:30-3:00							
3:00-3:30							
3:30-4:00							
4:00-4:30							
4:30-5:00							
5:00-5:30							
5:30-6:00							
6:00-6:30							
6:30-7:00							
7pm-7am							
TOTAL							
WEEK AVE.							

Form 22. Weekly, in Half-Hour Intervals (Home Observations). *Comments:* Interval or time sample recording. We often use this form for toileting, indicating W for wet, S for soiled, U for urinated in toilet, and BM for bowel movement in toilet.

CHECKLISTS ━━━

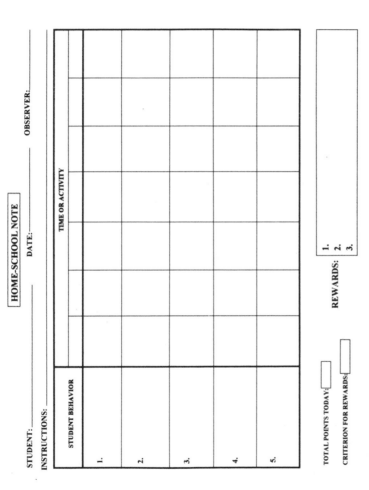

HOME-SCHOOL NOTE

STUDENT: _____   DATE: _____   OBSERVER: _____

INSTRUCTIONS: _____

STUDENT BEHAVIOR	TIME OR ACTIVITY						
1.							
2.							
3.							
4.							
5.							

TOTAL POINTS TODAY: ☐   REWARDS: 1.

CRITERION FOR REWARDS: ☐   2.

                                              3.

Form 23. Checklist (School Observations). *Comments:* For five behaviors across seven time periods. We usually have the teacher give a star or happy face for each task achieved (or acceptable behavior) in each interval. The form is then sent home and the child receives a reward based on a predetermined criterion. This is particularly useful for keeping communication open between school and home. This same form can be used at home for interval recording (e.g., keeping hands to self in 1-hour interval).

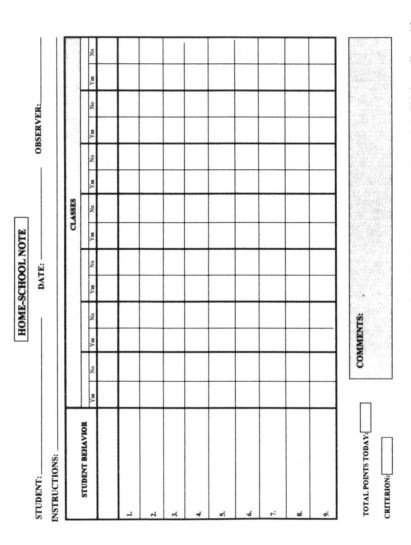

HOME-SCHOOL NOTE

STUDENT: _____   DATE: _____   OBSERVER: _____

INSTRUCTIONS:

STUDENT BEHAVIOR	CLASSES													
	Yes	No	Yes	No	Yes	No	Yes	No	Yes	No	Yes	No	Yes	No
1.														
2.														
3.														
4.														
5.														
6.														
7.														
8.														
9.														

TOTAL POINTS TODAY: [   ]

CRITERION: [   ]

COMMENTS:

Form 24. Checklist (School Observations). *Comments:* For nine behaviors across seven time periods. This is usually used for older students.

OUR WEEK
(_____ to _____)

	Monday	Tuesday	Wednesday	Thursday	Friday	Saturday	Sunday
A.M.							
P.M.							
TOTAL FOR DAY							

Form 25. Checklist (Home). *Comments:* This form can be used to write in home chores or behaviors for intervals of the day. We often use this form for pictograms.

RATING SCALES/QUALITY RECORDING

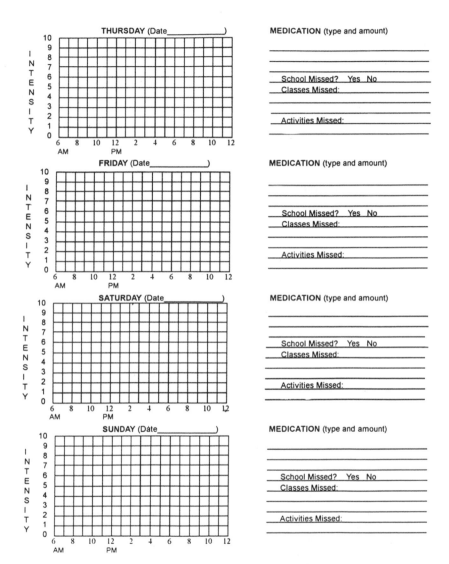

Form 26. Daily Pain Record. *Comments:* The form includes interval, duration, and intensity recording. The child is asked to rate his or her pain at any four times per day that he or she and the therapist agree upon (and any other times he or she wants) on the graph, then to note medication taken and activity changes due to pain. The points on the graph are then connected to show patterns of pain through the day. Points can be connected in a linear fashion (straight lines) or using curved lines to indicate variations between data points. The third page is usually kept during baseline only. (Thanks to Dr. Keith Allen for sharing this form with us.)

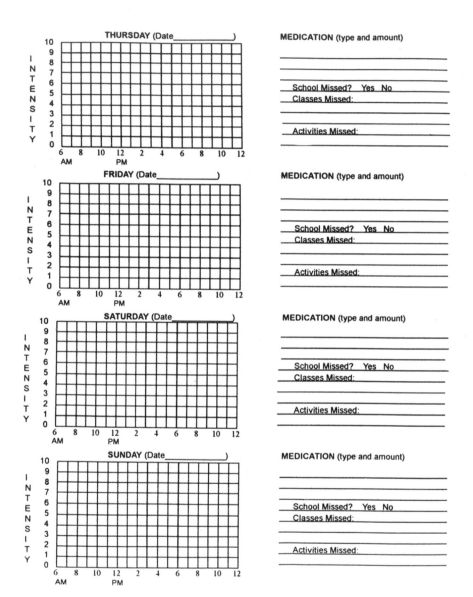

Form 26. (*Continued*)

Please put a check mark in front of each thing that happened before the pain occurred,
and each thing that happened after the pain occurred.

What Happened Before Pain?

☐ Ate something _____
Specify what _____
_____

☐ Drank something _____
Specify what _____
_____

☐ Glare or bright light
☐ Weather or temperature change
☐ Too much sleep
☐ Strong odors, fumes
☐ Game of competition
☐ Worried about something
☐ Sad/unhappy
☐ Difficult school work or test
☐ Angry about something
☐ Problem/fight with parents
☐ Problem/fight with friends
☐ Concentrated hard on something
☐ Something embarrassing happened
☐ Too much physical activity
☐ Woke up in morning with pain
☐ Woke up in night with pain
☐ Hunger
☐ I have my menstrual period (Day of period:_____)
☐ Other (please specify) _____
_____

What Happened During/After Pain?

☐ Took medication (indicate type and how much) ___
_____

☐ Missed school
☐ Missed one or more classes
Specify which class(es) _____
_____

☐ Did not complete homework
☐ Could not get out of bed in morning
☐ Chose a quiet activity to manage the pain
☐ Did not complete chores
Specify which chores missed _____
_____

☐ Missed practice/appointment/lesson.
Specify which practice/appointment(s) _____
_____

☐ Asked parent for help
☐ Asked parent for medication
☐ Tried to ignore pain
☐ Slept
☐ Rested
☐ Turned off lights, shut blinds, shades, or shutters
☐ Turned off sounds (T.V., music)
☐ Ate or drank something
☐ Applied heat/cold to pain location
☐ Massaged pain location
☐ Got a massage from someone else
☐ Started exercise or other recreation
☐ Cried
☐ Tried to distract self (listen to music, watch TV)
☐ Practiced relaxation
☐ Tried to remain active
☐ Did normal activity/routine
☐ Talked to parent/friend about pain
☐ Had a bowel movement
☐ Other (please specify) : _____
_____

Form 26. (*Continued*)

HOW WELL DID I DO?

NAME: _____ MONTH: _____ OBSERVER: _____

BEHAVIOR(S):_____

INSTRUCTIONS: 1. Write the date in the tiny box above the day of the week.
2. Under each number, write a descriptor e.g., 1= "great"; 2= "pretty good"....5= "needs work"
3. Check off the box that best describes your evaluation for the day and make any comments.

	1 =	2 =	3 =	4 =	5 =
SUNDAY					
MONDAY					
TUESDAY					
WEDNESDAY					
THURSDAY					
FRIDAY					
SATURDAY					
TOTAL					

Form 27. Likert Rating. *Comments:* Place date in shaded upper left-hand square. The clinician and parent/child should agree together on the descriptor used. This would be useful for rating the quality of a task.

| POSITIVE EVENTS AND PROBLEMS |

NAME: _____ WEEK :_____ OBSERVER: _____

INSTRUCTIONS: _____

	3 THINGS THAT _____ DID TODAY THAT I LIKED	ANY PROBLEMS THAT OCCURRED TODAY
☐ SUNDAY	1. _____ 2. _____ 3. _____	
☐ MONDAY	1. _____ 2. _____ 3. _____	
☐ TUESDAY	1. _____ 2. _____ 3. _____	
☐ WEDNESDAY	1. _____ 2. _____ 3. _____	
☐ THURSDAY	1. _____ 2. _____ 3. _____	
☐ FRIDAY	1. _____ 2. _____ 3. _____	
☐ SATURDAY	1. _____ 2. _____ 3. _____	

Form 28. Positive Events and Problems. *Comments:* This is particularly helpful for teaching parents (or teachers) to focus on positive behaviors in their child. If very negative or depressed, a child can also note his or her positive behaviors.

CHILD'S NAME:_____   DATE:_____

PERSON COMPLETING FORM:_____

Please take a few moments to let us know your opinion about the homework assignment from last session.

A. TARGETED PROBLEM:_____

	Not At all	Somewhat	Very Much
1. Did the behavior change since your last visit?	0	1	2
2. How useful were our suggestions?	0	1	2
3. How acceptable were our suggestions?	0	1	2
4. How useful was it to keep a record of the behavior?	0	1	2
5. How difficult was it to keep the record?	0	1	2

6. What difficulties did you have in
    following through on our
    recommendations?_____			

_____

_____

B. TARGETED PROBLEM:_____

	Not At all	Somewhat	Very Much
1. Did the behavior change since your last visit?	0	1	2
2. How useful were our suggestions?	0	1	2
3. How acceptable were our suggestions?	0	1	2
4. How useful was it to keep a record of the behavior?	0	1	2
5. How difficult was it to keep the record?	0	1	2

6. What difficulties did you have in
    following through on our
    recommendations?_____			

_____

_____

C. ARE THERE ANY OTHER PROBLEMS YOU WOULD LIKE TO DISCUSS TODAY?

_____

_____

_____

_____

Form 29. Acceptability of Measurement System. *Comments:* It is important to learn how effective our interventions are and how to make recording systems user-friendly. This form (or one similar to it) can be used to evaluate this at the end of treatment.

CUE-EFFECTIVENESS RECORDING

PERFORMANCE RECORD FORM

Child_____

Program:_____

IEP Goal #_____

Data Collection:

+   Correct
A+   Aprox
P+   Prompted
-    Incorrect
NR   No response

STEPS IN TASK:

1._____   6._____

2._____   7._____

3._____   8._____

4._____   9._____

5._____   10._____

TRIALS   **DAILY DATA SUMMARY**

Date	Time	Init	Step	1	2	3	4	5	6	7	8	9	10	# Trial	# +	% +	Comments

COMMENTS:

Form 30. Performance Record Form. *Comments:* Under "Training Steps," list steps in treatment (for example, a task analysis of a self-help skill or a step in discrimination training). For every 10 trials, mark the date, time, and initials of the person doing the training, the step in the training, the response for each trial, the number of trials conducted, the number correct, and the percent correct.

MISCELLANEOUS OTHER FORMS

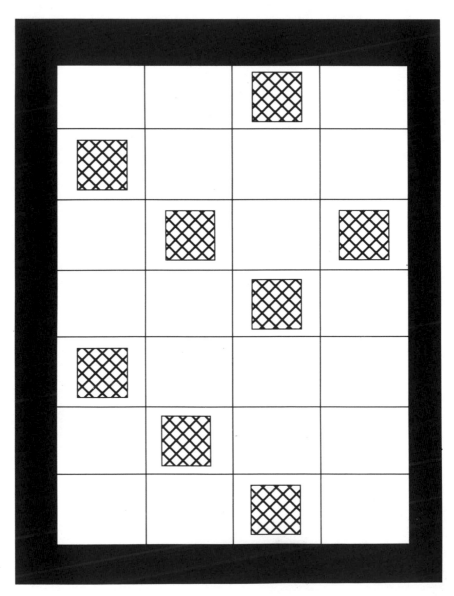

Form 31. Star Achievement Chart: Young Child. *Comments:* For intermittent reinforcement of performance of a young child. "Magic" squares are backed up with a larger reward (e.g., grab bag). Move across squares, left to right, and top to bottom.

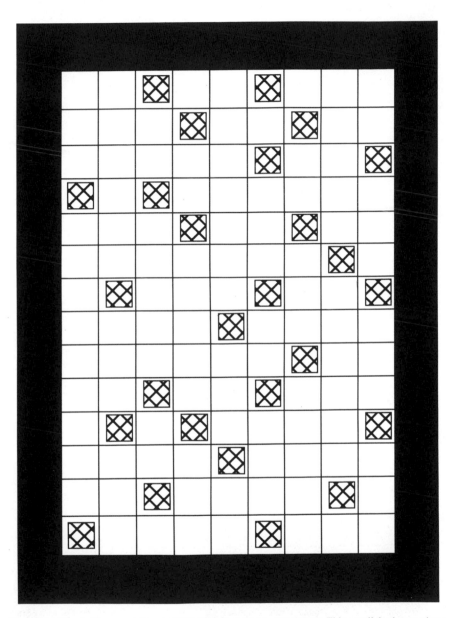

Form 32. Star Achievement Chart: Child Over 3–4 Years. *Comments:* This parallels the previous form, but has more squares so that it can be used for a longer time. Smaller stickers fit well in these squares.

TOKENS/POINTS

Name: _____   **PRIVILEGES:**

Points

Points

Form 33. Pictogram: Points or Tokens. *Comments:* Draw pictures of the privileges the child can earn for the varying points (denoted by the number of squares in the line). Then draw pictures of the required chores or behaviors at the bottom, with their point value underneath each picture. Generally, a new form should be used every day, with carryover points marked again on the next day.

Index